THE GAME OF LIFE
AND HOW TO PLAY IT
&
YOUR WORD IS YOUR WAND

REVIVE *classics*

The Game of Life and How to Play It & Your Word Is Your Wand
Shinn, Florence Scovel 1871 – 1940
The Game of Life and How to Play It
First Published by DeVorss & Company in 1925
Your Word Is Your Wand
First Published by DeVorss & Company in 1928

Text edits © 2024 Revive
Design © 2024 Revive

Text set in Adobe Caslon Pro.
Chapter headings set in Franklin Gothic.

All rights reserved. Generative artificial intelligence (AI) may have been used with both the text and artwork in this book. Human beings on our team do add their own creative edits to the text that is generated by AI. Humans also add other design elements to all images generated by AI. As such, all materials in this book are protected by copyright. No part of this publication may be reproduced, distributed, or transmitted in any form or by any means, including photocopying, recording, or other electronic or mechanical methods, without the prior written permission of the publisher or a licence from the Canadian Copyright Licensing Agency. Critics and reviewers may quote brief passages in connection with a review or critical article in any media.

Every reasonable effort has been made to contact the copyright holders of all material reproduced in this book.

ISBN: 978-1-998667-28-4

THE GAME OF LIFE
AND HOW TO PLAY IT
&
YOUR WORD IS YOUR WAND

FLORENCE SCOVEL SHINN

REVIVE

CONTENTS

The Game of Life and How to Play It

The Game   9

The Law of Prosperity   14

The Power of the Word   19

The Law of Nonresistance   24

The Law of Karma and the Law of Forgiveness   30

Casting the Burden (Impressing the Subconscious)   35

Love   39

Intuition or Guidance   45

Perfect Self-Expression or the Divine Design   51

Denials and Affirmations   57

Your Word Is Your Wand

Your Word Is Your Wand   67

Success Affirmations   69

Prosperity Affirmations   76

Happiness Affirmations   78

Love Affirmations   81

Marriage Affirmations   83

Forgiveness Affirmations   85

Words of Wisdom Affirmations   86

Faith Affirmations   90

Loss Affirmations   96

Debt Affirmations   98

Sales Affirmations   99

Interviews Affirmations   101

Guidance Affirmations   101

Protection Affirmations   103

Memory Affirmation   104

The Divine Design Affirmations   105

Health Affirmations   108

Eyes Affirmations   110

Anemia Affirmations   112

Ears Affirmations   113

Rheumatism Affirmations   114

False Growth Affirmations   115

Heart Disease Affirmations   116

Animals Affirmations   117

The Elements Affirmations   118

Journey Affirmation   120

Miscellaneous   121

Conclusion   127

The Game of Life
and How to Play It

"One secret
of her success was that
she was always herself... colloquial,
informal, friendly, and humorous.
She herself was very spiritual...
and taught by familiar, practical, and
everyday examples."

Emmet Fox

– On Florence Scovel Shinn –

The Game

Most people consider life a battle, but it is not a battle, it is a game.

It is a game, however, which cannot be played successfully without the knowledge of spiritual law, and the Old and the New Testaments give the rules of the game with wonderful clearness. Jesus Christ taught that it was a great game of *Giving and Receiving*.

"Whatsoever a man soweth that shall he also reap." This means that whatever man sends out in word or deed, will return to him; what he gives, he will receive.

If he gives hate, he will receive hate; if he gives love, he will receive love; if he gives criticism, he will receive criticism; if he lies he will be lied to; if he cheats he will be cheated. We are taught also, that the imaging faculty plays a leading part in the game of life.

"Keep thy heart (or imagination) with all diligence, for out of it are the issues of life." (Prov. 4:23.)

This means that what man images, sooner or later externalizes in his affairs. I know of a man who feared a certain disease. It was a very rare disease and difficult to get, but he pictured it continually and read about it until it manifested in his body, and he died, the victim of distorted imagination.

So we see, to play successfully the game of life, we must train the imaging faculty. A person with an imaging faculty trained to image only good, brings into his life "every righteous desire of his heart" – health, wealth, love, friends, perfect self-expression, his highest ideals.

The imagination has been called, "*The Scissors of The Mind,*" and it is ever cutting, cutting, day by day, the pictures man sees there, and sooner or later he meets his own creations in his outer world. To train the imagination successfully, man must understand the workings of his mind. The Greeks said: "Know Thyself."

There are three departments of the mind, the *subconscious, conscious and superconscious*. The subconscious, is simply power, without direction. It is like steam or electricity, and it does what it is directed to do; it has no power of induction.

Whatever man feels deeply or images clearly, is impressed upon the subconscious mind, and carried out in minutest detail.

For example: a woman I know, when a child, always "made believe" she was a widow. She "dressed up" in black clothes and wore a long black veil, and people thought she was very clever and amusing. She grew up and married a man with whom she was deeply in love. In a short time he died and she wore black and a sweeping veil for many years. The picture of herself as a widow was impressed upon the subconscious mind, and in due time worked itself out, regardless of the havoc created.

The conscious mind has been called mortal or carnal mind.

It is the human mind and sees life as it *appears to be*. It sees death, disaster, sickness, poverty and limitation of every kind, and it impresses the subconscious.

The *superconscious* mind is the God Mind within each man, and is the realm of perfect ideas.

In it, is the "*perfect pattern*" spoken of by Plato, *The Divine Design*; for there is a *Divine Design* for each person.

"*There is a place that you are to fill and no one else can fill, something you are to do, which no one else can do.*"

There is a perfect picture of this in the *superconscious mind*. It usually flashes across the conscious as an unattainable ideal – "something too good to be true."

In reality it is man's true destiny (or destination) flashed to him from the Infinite Intelligence which is *within himself*.

Many people, however, are in ignorance of their true destinies and are striving for things and situations which do not belong to them, and would only bring failure and dissatisfaction if attained.

For example: A woman came to me and asked me to "speak the word" that she would marry a certain man with whom she was very much in love. (She called him A. B.)

I replied that this would be a violation of spiritual law, but that I would speak the word for the right man, the "divine selection," the man who belonged to her by divine right.

I added, "If A. B. is the right man you can't lose him, and if he isn't, you will receive his equivalent." She saw A. B. frequently but no headway was made in their friendship. One evening she called, and said, "Do you know, for the last week, A. B. hasn't seemed so wonderful to me." I replied, "Maybe he is not the divine selection – another man may be the right one." Soon after that, she met another man who fell in love with her at once, and who said she was his ideal. In fact, he said all the things that she had always wished A. B. would say to her.

She remarked, "It was quite uncanny."

She soon returned his love, and lost all interest in A. B.

This shows the law of substitution. A right idea was substituted for a wrong one, therefore there was no loss or sacrifice involved.

Jesus Christ said, "Seek ye first the Kingdom of God and his righteousness; and all these things shall be added unto you," and he said the Kingdom *was within man.*

The Kingdom is the realm of *right ideas*, or the divine pattern.

Jesus Christ taught that man's words played a leading part in the game of life. "By your words ye are justified and by your words ye are condemned."

Many people have brought disaster into their lives through idle words.

For example: A woman once asked me why her life was now one of poverty of limitation. Formerly she had a home, was surrounded by beautiful things and had plenty of money. We found she had often tired of the management of her home, and had said repeatedly, "I'm sick and tired of things – I wish I lived in a trunk," and she added: "Today I am living in that trunk." She had spoken herself into a trunk. The subconscious mind has no sense of humor and people often joke themselves into unhappy experiences.

For example: A woman who had a great deal of money, joked continually about "getting ready for the poorhouse."

In a few years she was almost destitute, having impressed the subconscious mind with a picture of lack and limitation.

Fortunately the law works both ways, and a situation of lack may be changed to one of plenty.

For example: A woman came to me one hot summer's day for a "treatment" for prosperity. She was worn out, dejected and discouraged. She said she possessed just eight dollars in the world. I said, "Good, we'll bless the eight dollars and multiply them as Jesus Christ multiplied the loaves and the fishes," for He taught that every man had the power to bless and to multiply, to heal and to prosper.

She said, "What shall I do next?"

I replied, "Follow intuition. Have you a 'hunch' to do anything, or to go anywhere?" Intuition means, intuition, or to be taught from within.

It is man's unerring guide, and I will deal more fully with its laws in a following chapter.

The woman replied: "I don't know – I seem to have a 'hunch' to go home; I've just enough money for carfare." Her home was in a distant city and was one of lack and limitation, and the reasoning mind (or intellect) would have said: "Stay in New York and get work and make some money." I replied, "Then go home – never violate a hunch." I spoke the following words for her: "*Infinite Spirit open the way for great abundance for – –. She is an irresistible magnet for all that belongs to her by divine right.*" I told her to repeat it continually also. She left for home immediately. In calling on a woman one day, she linked up with an old friend of her family.

Through this friend, she received thousands of dollars in a most miraculous way. She has said to me often, "Tell people about the woman who came to you with eight dollars and a hunch."

There is always *plenty on man's pathway*, but it can only be *brought into manifestation* through desire, faith or the spoken word. Jesus Christ brought out clearly that man must make the *first move*.

"*Ask*, and it shall be given you, seek, and ye shall find, knock, and it shall be opened unto you. (Mat. 7:7.)

In the Scriptures we read:

"Concerning the works of my hands, command ye me."

Infinite Intelligence, God, is ever ready to carry out man's smallest or greatest demands.

Every desire, uttered or unexpressed, is a demand. We are often startled by having a wish suddenly fulfilled.

For example: One Easter, having seen many beautiful rose-trees in the florists' windows, I wished I would receive one, and for an instant saw it mentally being carried in the door.

Easter came, and with it a beautiful rose-tree. I thanked my friend the following day, and told her it was just what I had wanted.

She replied, "I didn't send you a rose-tree, I sent you lilies!"

The man had mixed the order, and sent me a rose-tree simply because I had started the law in action, and *I had to have a rose-tree.*

Nothing stands between man and his highest ideals and every desire of his heart, but doubt and fear. When man can "wish without worrying," every desire will be instantly fulfilled.

I will explain more fully in a following chapter the scientific reason for this and how fear must be erased from the consciousness. It is man's only enemy – fear of lack, fear of failure, fear of sickness, fear of loss and a feeling of *insecurity on some plane.* Jesus Christ said: "Why are ye fearful, oh ye of little faith?" (Mat. 8:26.) So we can see we must substitute faith for fear, for fear is only inverted faith; it is faith in evil instead of good.

The object of the game of life is to see clearly one's good and to obliterate all mental pictures of evil. This must be done by impressing the subconscious mind with a realization of good. A very brilliant man, who has attained great success, told me he had suddenly erased all fear from his consciousness by reading a sign which hung in a room. He saw printed, in large letters this statement – *"Why worry, it will probably never happen."* These words were stamped indelibly upon his subconscious mind, and he has now a firm conviction that only good can come into his life, therefore only *good can manifest.*

In the following chapter I will deal with the different methods of impressing the subconscious mind. It is man's faithful servant but one must be careful to give it the right orders. Man has ever a silent listener at his side – his subconscious mind.

Every thought, every word is impressed upon it and carried out in amazing detail. It is like a singer making a record on the sensitive disc of the phonographic plate. Every note and tone of the singer's voice is registered. If he coughs or hesitates, it is registered also. So let us break all the old bad records in the subconscious mind, the records of our lives which we do not wish to keep, and make new and beautiful ones.

Speak these words aloud, with power and conviction: "I now smash and demolish (by my spoken word) every untrue record in my subconscious mind. They shall return to the dust-heap of their native nothingness, for they came from my own vain imaginings. I now make my perfect records through the Christ within – The records of *Health, Wealth, Love and perfect self-Expression."* This is the square of life, The Game completed.

In the following chapters, I will show how man can *change his conditions by changing his words.* Any man who does not know the power of the word, is behind the times.

"Death and Life are in the power of the tongue."
(Prov. 18:21.)

The Law of Prosperity

*"Yea, the Almighty shall be thy defense
and thou shalt have plenty of silver."*

ONE OF THE GREATEST messages given to the race through the scriptures is that God is man's supply and that man can release, *through his spoken word*, all that belongs to him by divine right. He must, however, have *perfect faith in his spoken word*.

Isaiah said, "My word shall not return unto me void, but shall accomplish that where unto it is sent." We know now, that words and thoughts are a tremendous vibratory force, ever moulding man's body and affairs.

A woman came to me in great distress and said she was to be sued on the fifteenth of the month for three thousand dollars. She knew no way of getting the money and was in despair.

I told her God was her supply, and *that there is a supply for every demand*.

So *I spoke the word!* I gave thanks that the woman would receive three thousand dollars at the right time in the right way. I told her she must have perfect faith, and act her *perfect faith*. The fifteenth came but no money had materialized.

She called me on the 'phone and asked what she was to do.

I replied, "It is Saturday, so they won't sue you today. Your part is to act rich, thereby showing perfect faith that you will receive it by Monday." She asked me to lunch with her to keep up her courage. When I joined her at a restaurant, I said, "This is no time to economize. Order an expensive luncheon, act as if you have already received the three thousand dollars."

"All things whatsoever ye ask in prayer, believing, ye shall receive." "You must act as if you *had already received*." "The next morning she called me on the phone and asked me to stay with her during the day. I said "No, you are divinely protected and God is never too late."

In the evening she 'phoned again, greatly excited and said, "My dear, a miracle has happened! I was sitting in my room this morning, when the door-bell rang. I said to the maid: 'Don't let anyone in.' The maid however, looked out the window and said, 'It's your cousin with the long white beard.'

So I said, 'Call him back. I would like to see him.' He was just turning the corner, when he heard the maid's voice, and *he came back.*

He talked for about an hour, and just as he was leaving he said, 'Oh, by the way, how are finances?'

I told him I needed the money, and he said, 'Why, my dear, I will give you three thousand dollars the first of the month.'

I didn't like to tell him I was going to be sued. What shall I do? I won't *receive it till* the first of the month, and I must have it tomorrow." I said, "I'll keep on 'treating.'"

I said, "Spirit is never too late. I give thanks she has received the money on the invisible plane and that it manifests on time." The next morning her cousin called her up and said, "Come to my office this morning and I will give you the money." That afternoon, she had three thousand dollars to her credit in the bank, and wrote checks as rapidly as her excitement would permit.

If one asks for success and prepares for failure, he will get the situation he has prepared for. For example: A man came to me asking me to speak the word that a certain debt would be wiped out.

I found he spent his time planning what he would say to the man when he did not pay his bill, thereby neutralizing my words. He should have seen himself paying the debt.

We have a wonderful illustration of this in the bible, relating to the three kings who were in the desert, without water for their men and horses. They consulted the prophet Elisha, who gave them this astonishing message:

"Thus saith the Lord-Ye shall not see wind, neither shall ye see rain, yet make this valley full of ditches."

Man must prepare for the thing he has asked for, *when there isn't the slightest sign of it in sight.*

For example: A woman found it necessary to look for an apartment during the year when there was a great shortage of apartments in New York. It was considered almost an impossibility, and her friends were sorry for her and said, "Isn't it too bad, you'll have to store your furniture and live in a hotel." She replied, *"You needn't feel sorry for me, I'm a superman, and I'll get an apartment."*

She spoke the words: "*Infinite Spirit, open the way for the right apartment.*" She knew there was a supply for every demand, and that she was "unconditioned," working on the spiritual plane, and that "one with God is a majority."

She had contemplated buying new blankets, when "the tempter," the adverse thought or reasoning mind, suggested, "Don't buy the blankets, perhaps, after all, you won't get an apartment and you will have no use for them." She promptly replied (to herself): "I'll dig my ditches by buying the blankets!" So she prepared for the apartment – acted as though she already had it.

She found one in a miraculous way, and it was given to her although there were over *two hundred other applicants.*

The blankets showed active faith.

It is needless to say that the ditches dug by the three kings in the desert were filled to over-flowing. (Read, II Kings.)

Getting into the spiritual swing of things is no easy matter for the average person. The adverse thoughts of doubt and fear surge from the subconscious. They are the "army of the aliens" which must be put to flight. This explains why it is so often, "darkest before the dawn."

A big demonstration is usually preceded by tormenting thoughts.

Having made a statement of high spiritual truth one challenges the old beliefs in the subconscious, and "error is exposed" to be put out.

This is the time when one must make his affirmations of truth repeatedly, and rejoice and give thanks that he has already received. "Before ye call I shall answer." This means that "every good and perfect gift" is already man's awaiting his recognition.

Man can only receive what he sees himself receiving.

The children of Israel were told that they could have all the land they could see. This is true of every man. He has only the land within his own mental vision. Every great work, every big accomplishment, has been brought into manifestation through holding to the vision, and often just before the big achievement, comes apparent failure and discouragement.

The children of Israel when they reached the "Promised Land," were afraid to go in, for they said it was filled with giants who made them feel like grasshoppers. "And there we saw the giants and we were in our own sight as grasshoppers." This is almost every man's experience.

However, the one who knows spiritual law, is undisturbed by appearance, and rejoices while he is "yet in captivity." That is, he holds to his vision and gives thanks that the end is accomplished, he has received.

Jesus Christ gave a wonderful example of this. He said to his disciples: "Say not ye, there are yet four months and then cometh the harvest? Behold, I say unto you, lift up your eyes and look on the fields; for they are ripe already to harvest." His clear vision pierced the "world of matter" and he saw clearly the fourth dimensional world, things as they really are, perfect and complete in Divine Mind. So man must ever hold the vision of his journey's end and demand the manifestation of that which he has already received. It may be his perfect health, love, supply, self-expression, home or friends.

They are all finished and perfect ideas registered in Divine Mind (man's own superconscious mind) and must come through him, not to him. For example: A man came to me asking for treatments for success. It was imperative that he raise, within a certain time, fifty-thousand dollars for his business. The time limit was almost up, when he came to me in despair. No one wanted to invest in his enterprise, and the bank had flatly refused a loan. I replied: "I suppose you lost your temper while at the bank, therefore your power. You can control any situation if you first control yourself." "Go back to the bank," I added, "and I will treat." My treatment was: "You are identified in love with the spirit of everyone connected with the bank. Let the divine idea come out of this situation." He replied, "Woman, you are talking about an impossibility. Tomorrow is Saturday; the bank closes at twelve, and my train won't get me there until ten, and the time limit is up tomorrow, and anyway they won't do it. It's too late." I replied, "God doesn't need any time and is never too late. With Him all things are possible." I added, "I don't know anything about business, but I know all about God." He replied: "It all sounds fine when I sit here listening to you, but when I go out it's terrible." He lived in a distant city, and I did not hear from him for a week, then came a letter. It read: "You were right. I raised the money, and will never again doubt the truth of all that you told me."

I saw him a few weeks later, and I said, "What happened? You evidently had plenty of time, after all." He replied "My train was late, and I got there just fifteen minutes to twelve. I walked into the bank quietly and said, 'I have come for the loan,' and they gave it to me without a question."

It was the last fifteen minutes of the time allotted to him, and Infinite Spirit was not too late. In this instance the man could never have demonstrated alone. He needed someone to help him hold to the vision. This is what one man can do for another.

Jesus Christ knew the truth of this when he said: "If two of you shall agree on earth as touching anything that they shall ask, it shall be done for them of my Father which is in heaven." One gets too close to his own affairs and becomes doubtful and fearful.

The friend or "healer" sees clearly the success, health, or prosperity, and never wavers, because he is not close to the situation.

It is much easier to "demonstrate" for someone else than for one's self, so a person should not hesitate to ask for help, if he feels himself wavering.

A keen observer of life once said, "no man can fail, if some one person sees him successful." Such is the power of the vision, and many a great man has owed his success to a wife, or sister, or a friend who "believed in him" and held without wavering to the perfect pattern!

The Power of the Word

"By thy words thou shalt be justified, and by thy words thou shalt be condemned."

A PERSON KNOWING the power of the word, becomes very careful of his conversation. He has only to watch the reaction of his words to know that they do "not return void." Through his spoken word, man is continually making laws for himself.

I knew a man who said, "I always miss a car. It invariably pulls out just as I arrive."

His daughter said: "I always catch a car. It's sure to come just as I get there." This occurred for years. Each had made a separate law for himself, one of failure, one of success. This is the psychology of superstitions.

The horse-shoe or rabbit's foot contains no power, but man's spoken word and belief that it will bring him good luck creates expectancy in the subconscious mind, and attracts a "lucky situation." I find however, this will not "work" when man has advanced spiritually and knows a higher law. One cannot turn back, and must put away "graven images." For example: Two men in my class had had great success in business for several months, when suddenly everything "went to smash." We tried to analyze the situation, and I found, instead of making their affirmations and looking to God for success and prosperity, they had each bought a "lucky monkey." I said: "Oh I see, you have been trusting in the lucky monkeys instead of God." "Put away the lucky monkeys and call on the law of forgiveness," for man has power to forgive or neutralize his mistakes.

They decided to throw the lucky monkeys down a coalhole, and all went well again. This does not mean, however, that one should throw away every "lucky" ornament or horse-shoe about the house, but he must recognize that the power back of it is the one and only power, God, and that the object simply gives him a feeling of expectancy.

I was with a friend, one day, who was in deep despair. In crossing the street, she picked up a horseshoe. Immediately, she was filled with joy and hope. She said God had sent her the horseshoe in order to keep up her courage.

It was indeed, at that moment, about the only thing that could have registered in her consciousness. Her hope became faith, and she ultimately made a wonderful demonstration. I wish to make the point clear that the men previously mentioned were depending on the monkeys, alone, while this woman recognized the power back of the horse-shoe.

I know, in my own case, it took a long while to get out of a belief that a certain thing brought disappointment. If the thing happened, disappointment invariably followed. I found the only way I could make a change in the subconscious, was by asserting, "There are not two powers, there is only one power, God, therefore, there are no disappointments, and this thing means a happy surprise." I noticed a change at once, and happy surprises commenced coming my way.

I have a friend who said nothing could induce her to walk under a ladder. I said, "If you are afraid, you are giving in to a belief in two powers, Good and Evil, instead of one. As God is absolute, there can be no opposing power, unless man makes the false of evil for himself. To show you believe in only One Power, God, and that there is no power or reality in evil, walk under the next ladder you see." Soon after, she went to her bank. She wished to open her box in the safe-deposit vault, and there stood a ladder on her pathway. It was impossible to reach the box without passing under the ladder. She quailed with fear and turned back. She could not face the lion on her pathway. However, when she reached the street, my words rang in her ears and she decided to return and walk under it. It was a big moment in her life, for ladders had held her in bondage for years. She retraced her steps to the vault, and the ladder was no longer there! This so often happens! If one is willing to do a thing he is afraid to do, he does not have to.

It is the law of nonresistance, which is so little understood.

Someone has said that courage contains genius and magic. Face a situation fearlessly, and there is no situation to face; it falls away of its own weight.

The explanation is, that fear attracted the ladder on the woman's pathway, and fearlessness removed it.

Thus the invisible forces are ever working for man who is always "pulling the strings" himself, though he does not know it. Owing to the vibratory power of words, whatever man voices, he begins to attract. People who continually speak of disease, invariably attract it.

After man knows the truth, he cannot be too careful of his words. For example: I have a friend who often says on the 'phone, "Do come to see me and have a fine old-fashioned chat." This "old-fashioned chat" means an hour of about five hundred to a thousand destructive words, the principal topics being loss, lack, failure and sickness.

I reply: "No, I thank you, I've had enough old-fashioned chats in my life, they are too expensive, but I will be glad to have a new-fashioned chat, and talk about what we want, not what we don't want." There is an old saying that man only dares use his words for three purposes, to "heal, bless or prosper." What man says of others will be said of him, and what he wishes for another, he is wishing for himself.

"Curses, like chickens, come home to roost."

If a man wishes someone "bad luck," he is sure to attract bad luck himself. If he wishes to aid someone to success, he is wishing and aiding himself to success.

The body may be renewed and transformed through the spoken word and clear vision, and disease be completely wiped out of the consciousness. The metaphysician knows that all disease has a mental correspondence, and in order to heal the body one must first "heal the soul."

The soul is the subconscious mind, and it must be "saved" from wrong thinking.

In the twenty-third psalm, we read: "He restoreth my soul." This means that the subconscious mind or soul, must be restored with the right ideas, and the "mystical marriage" is the marriage of the soul and the spirit, or the subconscious and superconscious mind. They must be one. When the subconscious is flooded with the perfect ideas of the superconscious, God and man are one. "I and the Father are one." That is, he is one with the realm of perfect ideas; he is the man made in God's likeness and image (imagination) and is given power and dominion over all created things, his mind, body and affairs.

It is safe to say that all sickness and unhappiness come from the violation of the law of love. A new commandment I give unto you, "Love one another," and in the Game of Life, love or good-will takes every trick.

For example: A woman I know, had, for years an appearance of a terrible skin disease. The doctors told her it was incurable, and she was in despair. She was on the stage, and she feared she would soon have to give up her profession, and she had no other means of support. She, however, procured a good engagement, and on the opening night, made a great "hit." She received flattering notices from the critics, and was joyful and elated. The next day she received a notice of dismissal. A man in the cast had been jealous of her success and had caused her to be sent away. She felt hatred and resentment taking complete possession of her, and she cried out, "Oh God don't let me hate that man." That night she worked for hours "in the silence."

She said, "I soon came into a very deep silence. I seemed to be at peace with myself, with the man, and with the whole world. I continued this for two following nights, and on the third day I found I was healed completely of the skin disease!" In asking for love, or good will, she had fulfilled the law, ("for love is the fulfilling of the law") and the disease (which came from subconscious resentment) was wiped out.

Continual criticism produces rheumatism, as critical, inharmonious thoughts cause unnatural deposits in the blood, which settle in the joints.

False growths are caused by jealousy, hatred, unforgiveness, fear, etc. Every disease is caused by a mind not at ease. I said once, in my class, "There is no use asking anyone 'What's the matter with you?' we might just as well say, 'Who's the matter with you?'" Unforgiveness is the most prolific cause of disease. It will harden arteries or liver, and affect the eye-sight. In its train are endless ills.

I called on a woman, one day, who said she was ill from having eaten a poisoned oyster. I replied, "Oh, no, the oyster was harmless, you poisoned the oyster. What's the matter with you?" She answered, "Oh about nineteen people." She had quarrelled with nineteen people and had become so inharmonious that she attracted the wrong oyster.

Any inharmony on the external, indicates there is mental inharmony. "As the within, so the without."

Man's only enemies are within himself. "And a man's foes shall be they of his own household." Personality is one of the last enemies to be overcome, as this planet is taking its initiation in love. It was Christ's message – "Peace on Earth, good will towards man." The enlightened man, therefore, endeavors to perfect himself upon his neighbor. His work is with himself, to send out goodwill and blessings to every man, and the marvelous thing is, that if one blesses a man he has no power to harm him.

For example: A man came to me asking to "treat" for success in business. He was selling machinery, and a rival appeared on the scene with what he proclaimed, was a better machine, and my friend feared defeat. I said, "First of all, we must wipe out all fear, and know that God protects your interests, and that the divine idea must come out of the situation.

That is, the right machine will be sold, by the right man, to the right man." And I added, "Don't hold one critical thought towards that man. Bless him all day, and be willing not to sell your machine, if it isn't the divine idea." So he went to the meeting, fearless and nonresistant, and blessing the other man. He said the outcome was very remarkable. The other man's machine refused to work, and he sold his without the slightest difficulty. "But I say unto you, love your enemies, bless them that curse you, do good to them that hate you, and pray for them which spitefully use you and persecute you."

Good-will produces a great aura of protection about the one who sends it, and "No weapon that is formed against him shall prosper." In other words, love and good-will destroy the enemies within one's self, therefore, one has no enemies on the external!

"*There is peace on earth for him who sends good-will to man!*"

The Law of Nonresistance

"Resist not evil. Be not overcome of evil, but overcome evil with good."

Nothing on earth can resist an absolutely non-resistant person.

The Chinese say that water is the most powerful element, because it is perfectly nonresistant. It can wear away a rock, and sweep all before it.

Jesus Christ said, "Resist not evil," for He knew in reality, there is no evil, therefore nothing to resist. Evil has come of man's "vain imagination," or a belief in two powers, good and evil.

There is an old legend, that Adam and Eve ate of "Maya the Tree of Illusion," and saw two powers instead of one power, God.

Therefore, evil is a false law man has made for himself, through psychoma or soul sleep. Soul sleep means, that man's soul has been hypnotized by the race belief (of sin, sickness and death, etc.) which is carnal or mortal thought, and his affairs have out-pictured his illusions.

We have read in a preceding chapter, that man's soul is his subconscious mind, and whatever he feels deeply, good or bad, is outpictured by that faithful servant. His body and affairs show forth what he has been picturing. The sick man has pictured sickness, the poor man, poverty, the rich man, wealth.

People often say, "why does a little child attract illness, when it is too young even to know what it means?"

I answer that children are sensitive and receptive to the thoughts of others about them, and often outpicture the fears of their parents.

I heard a metaphysician once say, "If you do not run your subconscious mind yourself, someone else will run it for you."

Mothers often, unconsciously, attract illness and disaster to their children, by continually holding them in thoughts of fear, and watching for symptoms.

For example: A friend asked a woman if her little girl had had the measles. She replied promptly, "not yet!" This implied that she was expecting the illness, and, therefore, preparing the way for what she did not want for herself and child.

However, the man who is centered and established in right thinking, the man who sends out only good-will to his fellow-man, and who is without fear, cannot be *touched or influenced by the negative thoughts of others*. In fact, he could then receive only good thoughts, as he himself, sends forth only good thoughts.

Resistance is Hell, for it places man in a "state of torment."

A metaphysician once gave me a wonderful recipe for taking every trick in the game of life, it is the acme of nonresistance. He gave it in this way; "At one time in my life, I baptized children, and of course, they had many names. Now I no longer baptize children, but I baptize events, but *I give every event the same name.* If I have a failure I baptize it success, in the name of the Father, and of the Son, and of the Holy Ghost!"

In this, we see the great law of transmutation, founded on nonresistance. Through his spoken word, every failure was transmuted into success.

For example: A woman who required money, and who knew the spiritual law of opulence, was thrown continually in a business-way, with a man who made her feel very poor. He talked lack and limitation and she commenced to catch his poverty thoughts, so she disliked him, and blamed him for her failure. She knew in order to demonstrate her supply, she must first feel that she *had received – a feeling of opulence must precede its manifestation.*

It dawned upon her, one day, that she was resisting the situation, and seeing two powers instead of one. So she blessed the man and baptized the situation "Success"! She affirmed, "As there is only one power, God, this man is here for my good and my prosperity" (just what he did not seem to be there for). Soon after that she met, *through this man*, a woman who gave her for a service rendered, several thousand dollars, and the man moved to a distant city, and faded harmoniously from her life. Make the statement, "Every man is a golden link in the chain of my good," for all men are God in manifestation, *awaiting the opportunity given by man, himself, to serve the divine plan of his life.*

"Bless your enemy, and you rob him of his ammunition." His arrows will be transmuted into blessings.

This law is true of nations as well as individuals. Bless a nation, send love and good-will to every inhabitant, and it is robbed of its power to harm.

Man can only get the right idea of nonresistance, through spiritual understanding. My students have often said: "I don't want to be a doormat." I reply "when you use nonresistance with wisdom, no one will ever be able to walk over you."

Another example: One day I was impatiently awaiting an important telephone call. I resisted every call that came in and made no out-going calls myself, reasoning that it might interfere with the one I was awaiting.

Instead of saying, "Divine ideas never conflict, the call will come at the right time," leaving it to Infinite Intelligence to arrange, I commenced to manage things myself – I made the battle mine, not God's and remained tense and anxious. The bell did not ring for about an hour, and I glanced at the 'phone and found the receiver had been off that length of time, and the 'phone was disconnected. My anxiety, fear and belief in interference, had brought on a total eclipse of the telephone. Realizing what I had done, I commenced blessing the situation at once; I baptized it "success," and affirmed, "I cannot lose any call that belongs to me by divine right; I am under *grace, and not under law.*"

A friend rushed out to the nearest telephone, to notify the Company to reconnect.

She entered a crowded grocery, but the proprietor left his customers and attended to the call himself. My 'phone was connected at once, and two minutes later, I received a very important call, and about an hour afterward, the one I had been awaiting.

One's ships come in over a calm sea.

So long as man resists a situation, he will have it with him. If he runs away from it, it will run after him.

For example: I repeated this to a woman one day, and she replied, "How true that is! I was unhappy at home, I disliked my mother, who was critical and domineering; so I ran away and was married – but I married my mother, for my husband was exactly like my mother, and I had the same situation to face again." "Agree with thine adversary quickly."

That means, agree that the adverse situation is good, be undisturbed by it, and it falls away of its own weight. "None of these things move me," is a wonderful affirmation.

The inharmonious situation comes from some inharmony within man himself.

When there is, in him, no emotional response to an inharmonious situation, it fades away forever, from his pathway.

So we see man's work is ever with himself.

People have said to me, "Give treatments to change my husband, or my brother." I reply, "No, I will give *treatments to change you*; when you change, your husband and your brother will change."

One of my students was in the habit of lying. I told her it was a failure method and if she lied, she would be lied to. She replied, "I don't care, I can't possibly get along without lying."

One day she was speaking on the 'phone to a man with whom she was very much in love. She turned to me and said, "I don't trust him, I know he's lying to me." I replied, "Well, you lie yourself, so someone has to lie to you, and you will be sure it will be just the person you want the truth from." Some time after that, I saw her, and she said, "I'm cured of lying."

I questioned: "What cured you?"

She replied: "I have been living with a woman who lied worse than I did!"

One is often cured of his faults by seeing them in others.

Life is a mirror, and we find only ourselves reflected in our associates.

Living in the past is a failure method and a violation of spiritual law.

Jesus Christ said, "Behold, now is the accepted time." "Now is the day of Salvation."

Lot's wife looked back and was turned into a pillar of salt.

The robbers of time are the past and the future. Man should bless the past, and forget it, if it keeps him in bondage, and bless the future, knowing it has in store for him endless joys, but live *fully in the now*.

For example: A woman came to me, complaining that she had no money with which to buy Christmas gifts. She said, "Last year was so different; I had plenty of money and gave lovely presents, and this year I have scarcely a cent."

I replied, "You will never demonstrate money while you are pathetic and live in the past. Live fully in the *now*, and *get ready to give Christmas presents*. Dig your ditches, and the money will come." She exclaimed, "I know what to do! I will buy some tinsel twine, Christmas seals and wrapping paper." I replied, "Do that, and the *presents will come and stick themselves to the Christmas seals*."

This too, was showing financial fearlessness and faith in God, as the reasoning mind said, "Keep every cent you have, as you are not sure you will get any more."

She bought the seals, paper and twine, and a few days before Christmas, received a gift of several hundred dollars. Buying the seals and twine had impressed the subconscious with expectancy, and opened the way for the manifestation of the money. She purchased all the presents in plenty of time. Man must live suspended in the moment.

"Look well, therefore, to this Day! Such is the salutation of the Dawn."

He must be spiritually alert, ever awaiting his leads, taking advantage of every opportunity.

One day, I said continually (silently), "Infinite Spirit, don't let me miss a trick," and something very important was told to me that evening. It is most necessary to begin the day with right words.

Make an affirmation immediately upon waking. For example:

"*Thy will be done this day! Today is a day of completion; I give thanks for this perfect day, miracle shall follow miracle and wonders shall never cease.*"

Make this a habit, and one will see wonders and miracles come into his life.

One morning I picked up a book and read, "Look with wonder at that which is before you!" It seemed to be my message for the day, so I repeated again and again, "Look with wonder at that which is before you."

At about noon, a large sum of money, was given me, which I had been desiring for a certain purpose.

In a following chapter, I will give affirmations that I have found most effective. However, one should never use an affirmation unless it is absolutely satisfying and convincing to his own consciousness, and often an affirmative is changed to suit different people.

For example: The following has brought success to many:

"I have a wonderful work, in a wonderful way, I give wonderful service, for wonderful pay!"

I gave the first two lines to one of my students, and she added the last two.

It made a *most powerful statement*, as there should always be perfect payment for perfect service, and a rhyme sinks easily into the subconscious. She went about singing it aloud and soon did receive wonderful work in a wonderful way, and gave wonderful service for wonderful pay.

Another student, a business man, took it, and changed the word work to business.

He repeated, "I have a wonderful business, in a wonderful way, and I give wonderful service for wonderful pay." That afternoon he made a forty-one-thousand dollar deal, though there had been no activity in his affairs for months.

Every affirmation must be carefully worded and completely "cover the ground."

For example: I knew a woman, who was in great need, and made a demand for work. She received a great deal of work, but was never paid anything. She now knows to add, "wonderful service for wonderful pay."

It is man's divine right to have plenty! More than enough!

"His barns should be full, and his cup should flow over!" This is God's idea for man, and when man breaks down the barriers of lack in his own consciousness, the Golden Age will be his, and every righteous desire of his heart fulfilled!

The Law of Karma
and
The Law of Forgiveness

Man receives only that which he gives. The Game of Life is a game of boomerangs. Man's thoughts, deeds and words, return to him sooner or later, with astounding accuracy.

This is the law of Karma, which is Sanskrit for "Comeback." "Whatsoever a man soweth, that shall he also reap."

For example: A friend told me this story of herself, illustrating the law. She said, "I make all my Karma on my aunt, whatever I say to her, some one says to me. I am often irritable at home, and one day, said to my aunt, who was talking to me during dinner. *'No more talk, I wish to eat in peace.'*"

"The following day, I was lunching with a woman with whom I wished to make a great impression. I was talking animatedly, when she said: *'No more talk, I wish to eat in peace!'*"

My friend is high in consciousness, so her Karma returns much more quickly than to one on the mental plane.

The more man knows, the more he is responsible for, and a person with a knowledge of Spiritual Law, which he does not practice, suffers greatly, in consequence. "The fear of the Lord (law) is the beginning of wisdom." If we read the word Lord, law, it will make many passages in the Bible much clearer.

"Vengeance is mine, I will repay, saith the Lord" (law). It is the law which takes vengeance, not God. God sees man perfect, "created in his own image (imagination) and given "power and dominion."

This is the perfect idea of man, registered in Divine Mind, awaiting man's recognition; for man can only be what he sees himself to be, and only attain what he sees himself attaining.

"Nothing ever happens without an on-looker" is an ancient saying.

Man sees first his failure or success, his joy or sorrow, before it swings into visibility from the scenes set in his own imagination. We have observed this in the mother picturing disease for her child, or a woman seeing success for her husband.

Jesus Christ said, "And ye shall know the truth and the truth shall make you free."

So, we see freedom (from all unhappy conditions) comes through knowledge – a knowledge of Spiritual Law.

Obedience precedes authority, and the law obeys man when he obeys the law. The law of electricity must be obeyed before it becomes man's servant. When handled ignorantly, it becomes man's deadly foe. *So with the laws of Mind!*

For example: A woman with a strong personal will, wished she owned a house which belonged to an acquaintance, and she often made mental pictures of herself living in the house. In the course of time, the man died and she moved into the house. Several years afterwards, coming into the knowledge of Spiritual Law, she said to me: "Do you think I had anything to do with that man's death?" I replied: "Yes, your desire was so strong, everything made way for it, but you paid your Karmic debt. Your husband, whom you loved devotedly, died soon after, and the house was a white elephant on your hands for years."

The original owner, however, could not have been affected by her thoughts had he been positive in the truth, nor her husband, but they were both under Karmic law. The woman should have said (feeling the great desire for the house), "Infinite Intelligence, give me the right house, equally as charming as this, the house *which is mine by divine right.*"

The divine selection would have given perfect satisfaction and brought good to all. The divine pattern is the only safe pattern to work by.

Desire is a tremendous force, and must be directed in the right channels, or chaos ensues.

In demonstrating, the most important step is the *first step*, to *"ask aright."*

Man should always demand only that which is his by *divine right*.

To go back to the illustration: Had the woman taken this attitude: "If this house, I desire, is mine, I cannot lose it, if it is not, give me its equivalent," the man might have decided to move out, harmoniously (had it been the divine selection for her) or another house would have been substituted. Anything forced into manifestation through personal will, is always "ill-got," and has "ever bad success."

Man is admonished, "My will be done not thine," and the curious thing is, man always gets just what he desires when he does relinquish personal will, thereby enabling Infinite Intelligence to work through him.

"Stand ye still and see the salvation of the Lord" (law).

For example: A woman came to me in great distress. Her daughter had determined to take a very hazardous trip, and the mother was filled with fear.

She said she had used every argument, had pointed out the dangers to be encountered, and forbidden her to go, but the daughter became more and more rebellious and determined. I said to the mother, "You are forcing your personal will upon your daughter, which you have no right to do, and your fear of the trip is only attracting it, for man attracts what he fears." I added, "Let go, and take your mental hands off; *put it in God's Hands, and use this statement:*" "I put this situation in the hands of Infinite Love and Wisdom; if this trip is the Divine plan, I bless it and no longer resist, but if it is not divinely planned, I give thanks that it is now dissolved and dissipated. A day or two after that, her daughter said to her, "Mother, I have given up the trip," and the situation returned to its "native nothingness."

It is learning to "stand still," which seems so difficult for man. I have dealt more fully with this law in the chapter on nonresistance.

I will give another example of sowing and reaping, which came in the most curious way.

A woman came to me saying, she had received a counterfeit twenty-dollar bill, given to her at the bank. She was much disturbed, for, she said, "The people at the bank will never acknowledge their mistake."

I replied, "Let us analyze the situation and find out why you attracted it." She thought a few moments and exclaimed: "I know it, I sent a friend a lot of stagemoney, just for a joke." So the law had sent her some stage-money, for it doesn't know anything about jokes.

I said, "Now we will call on the law of forgiveness, and neutralize the situation."

Christianity is founded upon the law of forgiveness - Christ has redeemed us from the curse of the Karmic law, and the Christ within each man is his Redeemer and Salvation from all inharmonious conditions.

So I said: "Infinite Spirit, we call on the law of forgiveness and give thanks that she is under grace and not under law, and cannot lose this twenty dollars which is hers by divine right."

"Now," I said, "Go back to the bank and tell them, fearlessly, that it was given you, there by mistake."

She obeyed, and to her surprise, they apologized and gave her another bill, treating her most courteously.

So knowledge of the Law gives man power to "rub out his mistakes." Man cannot force the external to be what he is not.

If he desires riches, he must be rich first in consciousness.

For example: A woman came to me asking treatment for prosperity. She did not take much interest in her household affairs, and her home was in great disorder.

I said to her, "If you wish to be rich, you must be orderly. All men with great wealth are orderly – and order is heaven's first law." I added, "You will never become rich with a burnt match in the pincushion."

She had a good sense of humor and commenced immediately, putting her house in order. She rearranged furniture, straightened out bureau drawers, cleaned rugs, and soon made a big financial demonstration – a gift from a relative. The woman, herself, became made over, and keeps herself keyed-up financially, by being ever watchful of the *external and expecting prosperity, knowing God is her supply.*

Many people are in ignorance of the fact that gifts and things are investments, and that hoarding and saving invariably lead to loss.

"There is that scattereth and yet increaseth; and there is that withholdeth more than is meet, but it tendeth to poverty."

For example: I knew a man who wanted to buy a fur-lined overcoat. He and his wife went to various shops, but there was none he wanted. He said they were all too cheap-looking. At last, he was shown one, the salesman said was valued at a thousand dollars, but which the manager would sell him for five-hundred dollars, as it was late in the season.

His financial possessions amounted to about seven hundred dollars. The reasoning mind would have said, "You can't afford to spend nearly all you have on a coat," but he was very intuitive and never reasoned.

He turned to his wife and said, "If I get this coat, I'll make a ton of money!" So his wife consented, weakly.

About a month later, he received a ten-thousand-dollar commission. The coat made him feel so rich, it linked him with success and prosperity; without the coat, he would not have received the commission. It was an investment paying large dividends!

If man ignores these leadings to spend or to give, the same amount of money will go in an uninteresting or unhappy way.

For example: A woman told me, on Thanksgiving Day, she informed her family that they could not afford a Thanksgiving dinner. She had the money, but decided to save it.

A few days later, someone entered her room and took from the bureau drawer the exact amount the dinner would have cost.

The law always stands back of the man who spends fearlessly, with wisdom.

For example: One of my students was shopping with her little nephew. The child clamored for a toy, which she told him she could not afford to buy.

She realized suddenly that she was seeking lack, and not recognizing God as her supply!

So she bought the toy, and on her way home, picked *up, in the street, the exact amount of money she had paid for it.*

Man's supply is inexhaustible and unfailing when fully trusted, but faith or trust must precede the demonstration. "According to your faith be it unto you." "Faith is the substance of things hoped for, the evidence of things not seen – " for faith holds the vision steady, and the adverse pictures are dissolved and dissipated, and "in due season we shall reap, if we faint not."

Jesus Christ brought the good news (the gospel) that there was a higher law than the law of Karma – and that that law transcends the law of Karma. It is the law of grace, or forgiveness. It is the law which *frees man from the law of cause and effect – the law of consequence. "Under grace, and not under law."*

We are told that on this plane, man reaps where he has not sown; the gifts of God are simply poured out upon him. "All that the Kingdom affords is his." This continued state of bliss awaits the man who has overcome the race (or world) thought.

In the world thought there is tribulation, but Jesus Christ said: "Be of good cheer; I have overcome the world."

The world thought is that of sin, sickness and death. He saw their absolute unreality and said sickness and sorrow shall pass away and death itself, the last enemy, be overcome.

We know now, from a scientific standpoint, that death could be overcome by stamping the subconscious mind with the conviction of eternal youth and eternal life.

The subconscious, being simply power without direction, *carries out orders without questioning.*

Working under the direction of the superconscious (the Christ or God within man) the "resurrection of the body" would be accomplished.

Man would no longer throw off his body in death, it would be transformed into the "body electric," sung by Walt Whitman, for Christianity is founded upon the forgiveness of sins and "an empty tomb."

Casting the Burden

Impressing the Subconscious

When man knows his own powers and the workings of his mind, his great desire is to find an easy and quick way to impress the subconscious with good, for simply an intellectual knowledge of the Truth will not bring results.

In my own case, I found the easiest way is in "casting the burden."

A metaphysician once explained it in this manner. He said, "The only thing which gives anything weight in nature, is the law of gravitation, and if a boulder could be taken high above the planet, there would be no weight in that boulder; and that is what Jesus Christ meant when he said: "My yoke is easy and my burden is light."

He had overcome the world vibration, and functioned in the fourth dimensional realm, where there is only perfection, completion, life and joy.

He said: "Come to me all ye that labor and are heavy laden, and I will give you rest." "Take my yoke upon you, for my yoke is easy and my burden is light."

We are also told in the fifty-fifth Psalm, to "cast thy burden upon the Lord." Many passages in the Bible state that the battle is God's not man's and that man is always to "*stand still*" and *see the Salvation of the Lord*.

This indicates that the superconscious mind (or Christ within) is the department which fights man's battle and relieves him of burdens.

We see, therefore, that man violates law if he carries a burden, and a burden is an adverse thought or condition, and this thought or condition has its root in the subconscious.

It seems almost impossible to make any headway directing the subconscious from the conscious, or reasoning mind, as the reasoning mind (the intellect) is limited in its conceptions, and filled with doubts and fears.

How scientific it then is, to cast the burden upon the superconscious mind (or Christ within) where it is "made light," or dissolved into its "native nothingness."

For example: A woman in urgent need of money, "made light" upon the Christ within, the superconscious, with the statement, "I cast this burden of lack on the Christ (within) and I go free to have plenty!"

The belief in lack was her burden, and as she cast it upon the Superconscious with its belief of plenty, an avalanche of supply was the result.

We read, "The Christ in you the hope of glory."

Another example: One of my students had been given a new piano, and there was no room in her studio for it until she had moved out the old one. She was in a state of perplexity. She wanted to keep the old piano, but knew of no place to send it. She became desperate, as the new piano was to be sent immediately; in fact, was on its way, with no place to put it. She said it came to her to repeat, "I cast this burden on the Christ within, and I go free."

A few moments later, her 'phone rang, and a woman friend asked if she might rent her old piano, and it was moved out, a few minutes before the new one arrived.

I knew a woman, whose burden was resentment. She said, "I cast this burden of resentment on the Christ within, and I go free, to be loving, harmonious and happy." The Almighty superconscious, flooded the subconscious with love, and her whole life was changed. For years, resentment had held her in a state of torment and imprisoned her soul (the subconscious mind).

The statement should be made over and over and over, sometimes for hours at a time, silently or audibly, with quietness but determination.

I have often compared it to winding-up a victrola. We must wind ourselves up with spoken words. I have noticed, in "casting the burden," after a little while, one seems to see clearly. It is impossible to have clear vision, while in the throes of carnal mind. Doubts and fear poison the mind and body and imagination runs riot, attracting disaster and disease.

In steadily repeating the affirmation, "I cast this burden on the Christ within, and go free," the vision clears, and with it a feeling of relief, and sooner or later comes *the manifestation of good, be it health, happiness or supply.*

One of my students once asked me to explain the "darkness before the dawn." I referred in a preceding chapter to the fact that often, before the big demonstration "everything seems to go wrong," and deep depression clouds the consciousness. It means that out of the subconscious are rising the doubts and fears of the ages. These old derelicts of the subconscious rise to the surface, *to be put out*.

It is then, that man should clap his cymbals, like Jehoshaphat, and give thanks that he is saved, even though he seems surrounded by the enemy (the situation of lack or disease). The student continued, "How long must one remain in the dark" and I replied, "until one *can see in the dark*," and "*casting the burden enables one to see in the dark.*"

In order to impress the subconscious, active faith is always essential.

"Faith without works is dead." In these chapters I have endeavored to bring out this point.

Jesus Christ showed active faith when "He commanded the multitude to sit down on the ground," before he gave thanks for the loaves and the fishes.

I will give another example showing how necessary this step is. In fact, active faith is the bridge, over which man passes to his Promised Land.

Through misunderstanding, a woman had been separated from her husband, whom she loved deeply. He refused all offers of reconciliation and would not communicate with her in any way.

Coming into the knowledge of Spiritual law, she denied the appearance of separation. She made this statement: "There is no separation in Divine Mind, therefore, I cannot be separated from the love and companionship which are mine by divine right."

She showed active faith by arranging a place for him at the table every day; thereby impressing the subconscious with a picture of his *return*. Over a year passed, but she never wavered, and *one day he walked in*.

The subconscious is often impressed through music. Music has a fourth dimensional quality and releases the soul from imprisonment. It makes wonderful things seem *possible, and easy of accomplishment!*

I have a friend who uses her victrola, daily, for this purpose. It puts her in perfect harmony and releases the imagination.

Another woman often dances while making her affirmations. The rhythm and harmony of music and motion carry her words forth with tremendous power.

The student must remember also, not to despise the "day of small things."

Invariably, before a demonstration, come "signs of land."

Before Columbus reached America, he saw birds and twigs which showed him land was near. So it is with a demonstration; but often the student mistakes it for the demonstration itself, and is disappointed.

For example: A woman had "spoken the word" for a set of dishes. Not long afterwards a friend gave her a dish which was old and cracked.

She came to me and said, "Well, I asked for a set of dishes, and all I got was a cracked plate."

I replied, "The plate was only signs of land. It shows your dishes are coming – look upon it as birds and seaweed," and not long afterwards the dishes came.

Continually "making-believe," impresses the subconscious. If one makes believe he is rich, and makes believe he is successful, in "due time he will reap."

Children are always "making believe," and "except ye be converted, and become as little children, ye shall not enter the Kingdom of Heaven."

For example: I know of a woman who was very poor, but no one could make her *feel poor*. She earned a small amount of money from rich friends, who constantly reminded her of her poverty, and to be careful and saving. Regardless of their admonitions, she would spend all her earnings on a hat, or make someone a gift, and be in a rapturous state of mind. Her thoughts were always centered on beautiful clothes and "rings and things," but without envying others.

She lived in the world of the wondrous, and only riches seemed real to her. Before long she married a rich man, and the rings and things became visible. I do not know whether the man was the "Divine Selection," but opulence had to manifest in her life, as she had imaged only opulence.

There is no peace or happiness for man, until he has erased all fear from the subconscious.

Fear is misdirected energy and must be redirected, or transmuted into Faith.

Jesus Christ said, "Why are ye fearful, O ye of little faith?" "All things are possible to him that believeth."

I am asked, so often by my students, *"How can I get rid of fear?"*

I reply, *"By walking up to the thing you are afraid of."*

"The lion takes its fierceness from your fear."

Walk up to the lion, and he will disappear; run away and he runs after you.

I have shown in previous chapters, how the lion of lack disappeared when the individual spent money fearlessly, showing faith that God was his supply and therefore, unfailing.

Many of my students have come out of the bondage of poverty, and are now bountifully supplied, through losing all fear of letting money go out. The subconscious is impressed with the truth that *God is the Giver and the Gift;* therefore as one is one with the Giver, he is one with the Gift. A splendid statement is, "I now thank God the Giver for God the Gift."

Man hasso long separated himself from his good and his supply, through thoughts of separation and lack, that sometimes, it takes dynamite to dislodge these false ideas from the subconscious, and the dynamite is a big situation.

We see in the foregoing illustration, how the individual was freed from his bondage by *showing fearlessness.*

Man should watch himself hourly to detect if his motive for action is fear or faith.

"Choose ye this day whom we shall serve," fear or faith.

Perhaps one's fear is of personality. Then do not avoid the people feared; be willing to meet them cheerfully, and they will either prove "golden links in the chain of one's good," or disappear harmoniously from one's pathway.

Perhaps one's fear is of disease or germs. Then one should be fearless and undisturbed in a germ-laden situation, and he would be immune.

One can only contract germs while vibrating at the same rate as the germ, and fear drags men down to the level of the germ. Of course, the disease laden germ is the product of carnal mind, as all thought must objectify. Germs do not exist in the superconscious or Divine Mind, therefore are the product of man's "vain imagination."

"In the twinkling of an eye," man's release will come when he realizes *there is no power in evil.* The material world will fade away, and the fourth dimensional world, the "World of the Wondrous," will swing into manifestation.

"And I saw a new heaven, and a new earth – and there shall be no more death, neither sorrow nor crying, neither shall there be any more pain; for the former things are passed away."

LOVE

EVERY MAN on this planet is taking his initiation in love. "A new commandment I give unto you, that ye love one another." Ouspensky states, in "Tertium Organum," that "love is a cosmic phenomenon," and opens to man the fourth dimensional world, "The World of the Wondrous."

Real love is selfless and free from fear. It pours itself out upon the object of its affection, without demanding any return. Its joy is in the joy of giving. Love is God in manifestation, and the strongest magnetic force in the universe. Pure, unselfish love *draws to itself its own*; it does not need to seek or demand. Scarcely anyone has the faintest conception of real love. Man is selfish, tyrannical or fearful in his affections, thereby losing the thing he loves. Jealousy is the worst enemy of love, for the imagination runs riot, seeing the loved one attracted to another, and invariably these fears objectify if they are not neutralized.

For example: A woman came to me in deep distress. The man she loved had left her for other women, and said he never intended to marry her. She was torn with jealousy and resentment and said she hoped he would suffer as he had made her suffer; and added, "How could he leave me when I loved him so much?"

I replied, "You are not loving that man, you are hating him," and added, "*You can never receive what you have never given. Give a perfect love and you will receive a perfect love.* Perfect yourself on this man. Give him a perfect, *unselfish* love, demanding nothing in return, do not criticise or condemn, and *bless him wherever he is.*"

She replied, "No, I won't bless him unless I know where he is!"

"Well," I said, "that is not real love."

"When you *send out real love*, real love will return to you, either from this man or his equivalent, for if this man is not the divine selection, you will not want him. As you are one with God, you are one with the love which belongs to you by divine right."

Several months passed, and matters remained about the same, but she was working conscientiously with herself. I said, "When you are no longer disturbed by his cruelty, he will cease to be cruel, as you are attracting it through your own emotions."

Then I told her of a brotherhood in India, who never said, "Good morning" to each other. They used these words: "*I salute the Divinity in you.*" They saluted the divinity in every man, and in the wild animals in the jungle, and they were never harmed, for they *saw only God in every* living thing. I said, "Salute the divinity in this man, and say, 'I see your divine self only. I see you as God sees you, perfect, made in His image and likeness.'"

She found she was becoming more poised, and gradually losing her resentment. He was a Captain, and she always called him "The Cap."

One day, she said, suddenly, "*God bless the Cap wherever he is.*"

I replied: "Now, that is real love, and when you have become a 'complete circle,' and are no longer disturbed by the situation, you will have his love, or attract its equivalent."

I was moving at this time, and did not have a telephone, so was out of touch with her for a few weeks, when one morning I received a letter saying, "We are married."

At the earliest opportunity, I paid her a call. My first words were, "What happened?"

"Oh," she exclaimed, "a miracle! One day I woke up and all suffering had ceased. I saw him that evening and he asked me to marry him. We were married in about a week, and I have never seen a more devoted man."

There is an old saying: *"No man is your enemy, no man is your friend, every man is your teacher."*

So one should become impersonal and learn what each man has to teach him, and soon he would learn his lessons and be free.

The woman's lover was teaching her selfless love, which every man, sooner or later, must learn.

Suffering is not necessary for man's development; it is the result of violation of spiritual law, but few people seem able to rouse themselves from their "soul sleep" without it. When people are happy, they usually become selfish, and automatically the law of Karma is set in action. Man often suffers loss through lack of appreciation.

I knew a woman who had a very nice husband, but she said often, "I don't care anything about being married, but that is nothing against my husband. I'm simply not interested in married life."

She had other interests, and scarcely remembered she had a husband. She only thought of him when she saw him. One day her husband told her he was in love with another woman, and left. She came to me in distress and resentment.

I replied, "It is exactly what you spoke the word for. You said you didn't care anything about being married, so the subconscious worked to get you unmarried."

She said, "Oh yes, I see. People get what they want, and then feel very much hurt."

She soon became in perfect harmony with the situation, and knew they were both much happier apart.

When a woman becomes indifferent or critical, and ceases to be an inspiration to her husband, he misses the stimulus of their early relationship and is restless and unhappy.

A man came to me dejected, miserable and poor. His wife was interested in the "Science of Numbers," and had had him read. It seems the report was not very favorable, for he said, "My wife says I'll never amount to anything because I am a two."

I replied, "I don't care what your number is, you are a perfect idea in divine mind, and we will demand the success and prosperity which are *already planned* for you by that Infinite Intelligence."

Within a few weeks, he had a very fine position, and a year or two later, he achieved a brilliant success as a writer. No man is a success in business unless he loves his work. The picture the artist paints for love (of his art) is his greatest work. The pot-boiler is always something to live down.

No man can attract money if he despises it. Many people are kept in poverty by saying: "Money means nothing to me, and I have a contempt for people who have it."

This is the reason so many artists are poor. Their contempt for money separates them from it.

I remember hearing one artist say of another, "He's no good as an artist, he has money in the bank."

This attitude of mind, of course, separates man from his supply; he must be in harmony with a thing in order to attract it.

Money is God in manifestation, as freedom from want and limitation, but it must be always kept in circulation and put to right uses. Hoarding and saving react with grim vengeance.

This does not mean that man should not have houses and lots, stocks and bonds, for "the barns of the righteous man shall be full." It means man should not hoard even the principal, if an occasion arises, when money is necessary. In letting it go out fearlessly and cheerfully he opens the way for more to come in, for God is man's unfailing and inexhaustible supply.

This is the spiritual attitude towards money and the great Bank of the Universal never fails!

We see an example of hoarding in the film production of "Greed." The woman won five thousand dollars in a lottery, but would not spend it. She hoarded and saved, let her husband suffer and starve, and eventually she scrubbed floors for a living.

She loved the money itself and put it above everything, and one night she was murdered and the money taken from her.

This is an example of where "love of money is the root of all evil." Money in itself, is good and beneficial, but used for destructive purposes, hoarded and saved, or considered more important than love, brings disease and disaster, and the loss of the money itself.

Follow the path of love, and all things are added, *for God is love,* and *God is supply;* follow the path of selfishness and greed, and the supply vanishes, or man is separated from it.

For example; I knew the case of a very rich woman, who hoarded her income. She rarely gave anything away, but bought and bought and bought things for herself.

She was very fond of necklaces, and a friend once asked her how many she possessed. She replied, "Sixty-seven." She bought them and put them away, carefully wrapped in tissue paper. Had she used the necklaces it would have been quite legitimate, but she was violating "the law of use." Her closets were filled with clothes she never wore, and jewels which never saw the light.

The woman's arms were gradually becoming paralyzed from holding on to things, and eventually she was considered incapable of looking after her affairs and her wealth was handed over to others to manage.

So man, in ignorance of the law, brings about his own destruction.

All disease, all unhappiness, come from the violation of the law of love. Man's boomerangs of hate, resentment and criticism, come back laden with sickness and sorrow. Love seems almost a lost art, but the man with the knowledge of spiritual law knows it must be regained, for without it, he has "become as sounding brass and tinkling cymbals."

For example: I had a student who came to me, month after month, to clean her consciousness of resentment. After a while, she arrived at the point where she resented only one woman, but that one woman kept her busy. Little by little she became poised and harmonious, and one day, all resentment was wiped out.

She came in radiant, and exclaimed "You can't understand how I feel! The woman said something to me and instead of being furious I was loving and kind, and she apologized and was perfectly lovely to me.

No one can understand the marvelous lightness I feel within!"

Love and good-will are invaluable in business.

For example: A woman came to me, complain ing of her employer. She said she was cold and critical and knew she did not want her in the position.

"Well," I replied, "Salute the Divinity in the woman and send her love."

She said "I can't; she's a marble woman."

I answered, "You remember the story of the sculptor who asked for a certain piece of marble. He was asked why he wanted it, and he replied, 'because there is an angel in the marble,' and out of it he produced a wonderful work of art."

She said, "Very well, I'll try it." A week later she came back and said, "I did what you told me to, and now the woman is very kind, and took me out in her car."

People are sometimes filled with remorse for having done someone an unkindness, perhaps years ago.

If the wrong cannot be righted, its effect can be neutralized by doing some one a kindness *in the present.*

"This one thing I do, forgetting those things which are behind and reaching forth unto those things which are before."

Sorrow, regret and remorse tear down the cells of the body, and poison the atmosphere of the individual.

A woman said to me in deep sorrow, "Treat me to be happy and joyous, for my sorrow makes me so irritable with the members of my family that I keep making more Karma."

I was asked to treat a woman who was mourning for her daughter. I denied all belief in loss and separation, and affirmed that God was the woman's joy, love and peace.

The woman gained her poise at once, but sent word by her son, not to treat any longer, because she was "so happy, it wasn't respectable."

So "mortal mind" loves to hang on to its griefs and regrets.

I knew a woman who went about bragging of her troubles, so, of course, she always had something to brag about.

The old idea was if a woman did not worry about her children, she was not a good mother.

Now, we know that mother-fear is responsible for many of the diseases and accidents which come into the lives of children.

For fear pictures vividly the disease or situation feared, and these pictures objectify, if not neutralized.

Happy is the mother who can say sincerely, that she puts her child in God's hands, and *knows* therefore, that he is divinely protected.

For example: A woman awoke suddenly, in the night, feeling her brother was in great danger. Instead of giving in to her fears, she commenced making statements of Truth, saying, "Man is a perfect idea in Divine Mind, and is always in his right place, therefore, my brother is in his right place, and is divinely protected."

The next day she found that her brother had been in close proximity to an explosion in a mine, but had miraculously escaped.

So man is his brother's keeper (in thought) and every man should know that the thing he loves dwells in "the secret place of the most high, and abides under the shadow of the Almighty."

"There shall no evil befall thee, neither shall any plague come nigh thy dwelling."

"Perfect love casteth out fear. He that feareth is not made perfect in love," and "Love is the fulfilling of the Law."

Intuition or Guidance

"In all thy ways acknowledge Him and
He shall direct thy paths."

There is nothing too great of accomplishment for the man who knows the power of his word, and who follows his intuitive leads. By the word he starts in action unseen forces and can rebuild his body or remold his affairs.

It is, therefore, of the utmost importance to choose the right words, and the student carefully selects the affirmation he wishes to catapult into the invisible.

He knows that God is his supply, that there is a supply for every demand, and that his spoken word releases this supply.

"Ask and ye shall receive."

Man must make the first move. "Draw nigh to God and He will draw nigh to you."

I have often been asked just how to make a demonstration.

I reply: "Speak the word and then do not do anything until you get a definite lead." Demand the lead, saying, "Infinite Spirit, reveal to me the way, let me know if there is anything for me to do."

The answer will come through intuition (or hunch); a chance remark from someone, or a passage in a book, etc., etc. The answers are sometimes quite startling in their exactness. For example: A woman desired a large sum of money. She spoke the words: "Infinite Spirit, open the way for my immediate supply, let all that is mine by divine right now reach me, in great avalanches of abundance." Then she added: "Give me a definite lead, let me know if there is anything for me to do."

The thought came quickly, "Give a certain friend" (who had helped her spiritually) "a hundred dollars." She told her friend, who said, "Wait and get another lead, before giving it." So she waited, and that day met a woman who said to her, "I gave someone a dollar today; it was just as much for me, as it would be for you to give someone a hundred."

This was indeed an unmistakable lead, so she knew she was right in giving the hundred dollars. It was a gift which proved a great investment, for shortly after that, a large sum of money came to her in a remarkable way.

Giving opens the way for receiving. In order to create activity in finances, one should give. Tithing or giving one-tenth of one's income, is an old Jewish custom, and is sure to bring increase. Many of the richest men in this country have been tithers, and I have never known it to fail as an investment.

The tenth-part goes forth and returns blessed and multiplied. But the gift or tithe must be given with love and cheerfulness, for "God loveth a cheerful giver." Bills should be paid cheerfully; all money should be sent forth fearlessly and with a blessing.

This attitude of mind makes man master of money. It is his to obey, and his spoken word then opens vast reservoirs of wealth.

Man, himself, limits his supply by his limited vision. Sometimes the student has a great realization of wealth, but is afraid to act.

The vision and action must go hand in hand, as in the case of the man who bought the fur-lined overcoat.

A woman came to me asking me to "speak the word" for a position. So I demanded: "Infinite Spirit, open the way for this woman's right position." Never ask for just "a position"; ask for the right position, the place already planned in Divine Mind, as it is the only one that will give satisfaction.

I then gave thanks that she had already received, and that it would manifest quickly. Very soon, she had three positions offered her, two in New York and one in Palm Beach, and she did not know which to choose. I said, "Ask for a definite lead."

The time was almost up and was still undecided, when one day, she telephoned, "When I woke up this morning, I could smell Palm Beach." She had been there before and knew its balmy fragrance.

I replied: "Well, if you can smell Palm Beach from here, it is certainly your lead." She accepted the position, and proved a great success. Often one's lead comes at an unexpected time.

One day, I was walking down the street, when I suddenly felt a strong urge to go to a certain bakery, a block or two away.

The reasoning mind resisted, arguing, "There is nothing there that you want."

However, I had learned not to reason, so I went to the bakery, looked at everything, and there was certainly nothing there that I wanted, but coming out I encountered a woman I had thought of often, and who was in great need of the help which I could give her.

So often, one goes for one thing and finds another.

Intuition is a spiritual faculty and does not explain, but simply *points the way.*

A person often receives a lead during a "treatment." The idea that comes may seem quite irrelevant, but some of God's leadings are "mysterious."

In the class, one day, I was treating that each individual would receive a definite lead. A woman came to me afterwards, and said: "While you were treating, I got the hunch to take my furniture out of storage and get an apartment." The woman had come to be treated for health. I told her I knew in getting a home of her own, her health would improve, and I added, "I believe your trouble, which is a congestion, has come from having things stored away. Congestion of things causes congestion in the body. You have violated the law of use, and your body is paying the penalty."

So I gave thanks that *"Divine order was established in her mind, body and affairs."*

People little dream of how their affairs react on the body. There is a mental correspondence for every disease. A person might receive instantaneous healing through the realization of his body being a perfect idea in Divine Mind, and, therefore, whole and perfect, but if he continues his destructive thinking, hoarding, hating, fearing, condemning, the disease will return.

Jesus Christ knew that all sickness came from sin, but admonished the leper after the healing, to go and sin no more, lest a worse thing come upon him.

So man's soul (or subconscious mind) must be washed whiter than snow, for permanent healing; and the metaphysician is always delving deep for the "correspondence."

Jesus Christ said, "Condemn not lest ye also be condemned."

"Judge not, lest ye be judged."

Many people have attracted disease and unhappiness through condemnation of others.

What man condemns in others, he attracts to himself.

For example: A friend came to me in anger and distress, because her husband had deserted her for another woman. She condemned the other woman, and said continually, "She knew he was a married man, and had no right to accept his attentions."

I replied. "Stop condemning the woman, bless her, and be through with the situation, otherwise, you are attracting the same thing to yourself."

She was deaf to my words, and a year or two later, became deeply interested in a married man, herself.

Man picks up a live-wire whenever he criticises or condemns, and may expect a shock.

Indecision is a stumbling-block in many a path way. In order to overcome it, make the statement, repeatedly, *"I am always under direct inspiration; I make right decisions, quickly."*

These words impress the subconscious, and soon one finds himself awake and alert, making his right moves without hesitation. I have found it destructive to look to the psychic plane for guidance, as it is the plane of many minds and not "The One Mind."

As man opens his mind to subjectivity, he becomes a target for destructive forces. The psychic plane is the result of man's mortal thought, and is on the "plane of opposites." He may receive either good or bad messages.

The science of numbers and the reading of horoscopes, keep man down on the mental (or mortal) plane, for they deal only with the Karmic path.

I know of a man who should have been dead, years ago, according to his horoscope, but he is alive and a leader of one of the biggest movements in this country for the uplift of humanity.

It takes a very strong mind to neutralize a prophecy of evil. The student should declare, "Every false prophecy shall come to naught; every plan my Father in heaven has not planned, shall be dissolved and dissipated, the divine idea now comes to pass."

However, if any good message has ever been given one, of coming happiness, or wealth, harbor and expect it, and it will manifest sooner or later, through the law of expectancy.

Man's will should be used to back the universal will. "I will that the will of God be done."

It is God's will to give every man, every righteous desire of his heart, and man's will should be used to hold the perfect vision, without wavering.

The prodigal son said: "I will arise and go to my Father."

It is, indeed, often an effort of the will to leave the husks and swine of mortal thinking. It is so much easier, for the average person, to have fear than faith; *so faith is an effort of the will.*

As man becomes spiritually awakened he recognizes that any external inharmony is the correspondence of mental inharmony. If he stumbles or falls, he may know he is stumbling or falling in consciousness.

One day, a student was walking along the street condemning someone in her thoughts. She was saying, mentally, "That woman is the most disagreeable woman on earth," when suddenly three boy scouts rushed around the corner and almost knocked her over. She did not condemn the boy scouts, but immediately called on the law of forgiveness, and "saluted the divinity" in the woman. Wisdom's way are ways of pleasantness and all her paths are peace.

When one has made his demands upon the Universal, he must be ready for surprises. Everything may seem to be going wrong, when in reality, it is going right.

For example: A woman was told that there was no loss in divine mind, therefore, she could not lose anything which belonged to her; anything lost, would be returned, or she would receive its equivalent.

Several years previously, she had lost two thousand dollars. She had loaned the money to a relative during her lifetime, but the relative had died, leaving no mention of it in her will. The woman was resentful and angry, and as she had no written statement of the transaction, she never received the money, so she determined to deny the loss, and collect the two thousand dollars from the Bank of the Universal. She had to begin by forgiving the woman, as resentment and unforgiveness close the doors of this wonderful bank.

She made this statement, "I deny loss, there is no loss in Divine Mind, therefore, I cannot lose the two thousand dollars, which belong to me by divine right. *As one door shuts another door opens.*"

She was living in an apartment house which was for sale; and in the lease was a clause, stating that if the house was sold, the tenants would be required to move out within ninety days.

Suddenly, the landlord broke the leases and raised the rent. Again, injustice was on her pathway, but this time she was undisturbed. She blessed the landlord, and said, "As the rent has been raised, it means that I'll be that much richer, for God is my supply."

New leases were made out for the advanced rent, but by some divine mistake, the ninety days clause had been forgotten. Soon after, the landlord had an opportunity to sell the house. On account of the mistake in the new leases, the tenants held possession for another year.

The agent offered each tenant two hundred dollars if he would vacate. Several families moved; three remained, including the woman. A month or two passed, and the agent again appeared. This time he said to the woman, "Will you break your lease for the sum of fifteen hundred dollars?" It flashed upon her, "Here comes the two thousand dollars." She remembered having said to friends in the house, "We will all act together if anything more is said about leaving." So her *lead* was to consult her friends.

These friends said: "Well, if they have offered you fifteen hundred they will certainly give two thousand." So she received a check for two thousand dollars for giving up the apartment. It was certainly a remarkable working of the law, and the apparent injustice was merely opening the way for her demonstration.

It proved that there is no loss, and when man takes his spiritual stand, he collects all that is his from this great Reservoir of Good.

"I will restore to you the years the locusts have eaten."

The locusts are the doubts, fears, resentments and regrets of mortal thinking.

These adverse thoughts, alone, rob man; for "No man gives to himself but himself, and no man takes away from himself, but himself."

Man is here to prove God and "to bear witness to the truth," and he can only prove God by bringing plenty out of lack, and justice out of injustice.

"Prove me now herewith, saith the Lord of hosts, if I will not open you the windows of heaven, and pour out a blessing, that there shall not be room enough to receive it."

Perfect Self-Expression
or
The Divine Design

"No wind can drive my bark astray
nor change the tide of destiny."

THERE IS FOR EACH MAN, perfect self-expression. There is a place which he is to fill and no one else can fill, something which he is to do, which no one else can do; it is his destiny!

This achievement is held, a perfect idea in Divine Mind, awaiting man's recognition. As the imaging faculty is the creative faculty, it is necessary for man to see the idea, before it can manifest.

So man's highest demand is for the *Divine Design of his life.*

He may not have the faintest conception of what it is, for there is, possibly, some marvelous talent, hidden deep within him.

His demand should be: "*Infinite Spirit, open the way for the Divine Design of my life to manifest; let the genius within me now be released; let me see clearly the perfect plan.*"

The perfect plan includes health, wealth, love and perfect self-expression. This is the *square of life*, which brings perfect happiness. When one has made this demand, he may find great changes taking place in his life, for nearly every man has wandered far from the Divine Design.

I know, in one woman's case, it was as though a cyclone had struck her affairs, but readjustments came quickly, and new and wonderful conditions took the place of old ones.

Perfect self-expression will never be labor; but of such absorbing interest that it will seem almost like play. The student knows, also, as man comes into the world financed by God, the *supply* needed for his perfect self-expression will be at hand.

Many a genius has struggled for years with the problem of supply, when his spoken word, and faith, would have released quickly, the necessary funds.

For example: After the class, one day, a man came to me and handed me a cent.

He said: "I have just seven cents in the world, and I'm going to give you one; for I have faith in the power of your spoken word. I want you to speak the word for my perfect self-expression and prosperity."

I "spoke the word," and did not see him again until a year later. He came in one day, successful and happy, with a roll of yellow bills in his pocket. He said, "Immediately after you spoke the word, I had a position offered me in a distant city, and am now demonstrating health, happiness and supply."

A woman's perfect self-expression may be in becoming a perfect wife, a perfect mother, a perfect home-maker and not necessarily in having a public career.

Demand definite leads, and the way will be made easy and successful.

One should not visualize or force a mental picture. When he demands the Divine Design to come into his conscious mind, he will receive flashes of inspiration, and begin to see himself making some great accomplishment. This is the picture, or idea, he must hold without wavering.

The thing man seeks is seeking him – *the telephone was seeking Bell!*

Parents should never force careers and professions upon their children. With a knowledge of spiritual Truth, the Divine Plan could be spoken for, early in childhood, or prenatally.

A prenatal treatment should be: "Let the God in this child have perfect expression; let the Divine Design of his mind, body and affairs be made manifest throughout his life, throughout eternity."

God's will be done, not man's; God's pattern, not man's pattern, is the command we find running through all the scriptures, and the Bible is a book dealing with the science of the mind. It is a book telling man how to release his soul (or subconscious mind) from bondage.

The battles described are pictures of man waging war against mortal thoughts. "A man's foes shall be they of his own household." Every man is Jehoshaphat, and every man is David, who slays Goliath (mortal thinking) with the little white stone (faith).

So man must be careful that he is not the "wicked and slothful servant" who buried his talent. There is a terrible penalty to be paid for not using one's ability.

Often fear stands between man and his perfect self-expression. Stage-fright has hampered many a genius. This may be overcome by the spoken word, or treatment. The individual then loses all self-consciousness, and feels simply that he is a channel for Infinite Intelligence to express Itself through.

He is under direct inspiration, fearless, and confident; for he feels that it is the "Father within" him who does the work.

A young boy came often to my class with his mother. He asked me to "speak the word" for his coming examinations at school.

I told him to make the statement: "I am one with Infinite Intelligence. I know everything I should know on this subject." He had an excellent knowledge of history, but was not sure of his arithmetic. I saw him afterwards, and he said: "I spoke the word for my arithmetic, and passed with the highest honors; but thought I could depend on myself for history, and got a very poor mark." Man often receives a set-back when he is "too sure of himself," which means he is trusting to his personality and not the "Father within."

Another one of my students gave me an example of this. She took an extended trip abroad one summer, visiting many countries, where she was ignorant of the languages. She was calling for guidance and protection every minute, and her affairs went smoothly and miraculously. Her luggage was never delayed nor lost! Accommodations were always ready for her at the best hotels; and she had perfect service wherever she went. She returned to New York. Knowing the language, she felt God was no longer necessary, so looked after her affairs in an ordinary manner.

Everything went wrong, her trunks delayed, amid inharmony and confusion. The student must form the habit of "practicing the Presence of God" every minute. "*In all thy ways acknowledge him;*" nothing is too small or too great.

Sometimes an insignificant incident may be the turning point in a man's life.

Robert Fulton, watching some boiling water, simmering in a tea kettle, saw a steamboat!

I have seen a student, often, keep back his demonstration, through resistance, or pointing the way.

He pins his faith to one channel only, and dictates just the way he desires the manifestation to come, which brings things to a standstill.

"*My way, not your way!*" is the command of Infinite Intelligence. Like all Power, be it steam or electricity, it must have a nonresistant engine or instrument to work through, and man is that engine or instrument.

Over and over again, man is told to "stand still". "Oh Judah, fear not; but to-morrow go out against them, for the Lord will be with you. You shall not need to fight this battle; set yourselves, stand ye still, and see the salvation of the Lord with you."

We see this in the incidents of the two thousand dollars coming to the woman through the landlord when she became *nonresistant* and *undisturbed,* and the woman who won the man's love "after all suffering had ceased."

The student's goal is *Poise! Poise is Power*, for it gives God-Power chance to rush through man, to "will and to do Its good pleasure."

Poised, he thinks clearly, and makes "right decisions quickly." "He never misses a trick."

Anger blurs the visions, poisons the blood, is the root of many diseases, and causes wrong decision leading to failure.

It has been named one of the worst "sins," as its reaction is so harmful. The student learns that in metaphysics sin has a much broader meaning than in the old teaching. "Whatsoever is not of faith is sin."

He finds that fear and worry are deadly sins. They are inverted faith, and through distorted mental pictures, bring to pass the thing he fears. His work is to drive out these enemies (from the subconscious mind). "When Man is *fearless he is finished!*" Maeterlinck says, that "Man is God afraid."

So, as we read in the previous chapters: Man can only vanquish fear by walking up to the thing he is afraid of. When Jehoshaphat and his army prepared to meet the enemy, singing "Praise the Lord, for his mercy endureth forever," they found their enemies had destroyed each other, and there was nothing to fight.

For example: A woman asked a friend to deliver a message to another friend. The woman feared to give the message, as the reasoning mind said, "Don't get mixed-up in this affair, don't give that message."

She was troubled in spirit, for she had given her promise. At last, she determined to "walk up to the lion," and call on the law of divine protection. She met the friend to whom she was to deliver the message. She opened her mouth to speak it, when her friend said, "So-and-So has left town." This made it unnecessary to give the message, as the situation depended upon the person being in town. As she was willing to do it, she was not obliged to; as she did not fear, the situation vanished.

The student often delays his demonstration through a belief in incompletion. He should make this statement:

"In Divine Mind there is only completion, therefore, my demonstration is completed. My perfect work, my perfect home, my perfect health."

Whatever he demands are perfect ideas registered in Divine Mind, and must manifest, "under grace in a perfect way." He gives thanks he has already received on the invisible, and makes active preparation for receiving on the visible.

One of my students was in need of a financial demonstration. She came to me and asked why it was not completed.

I replied: "Perhaps, you are in the habit of leaving things unfinished, and the subconscious has gotten into the habit of not completing (as the without, so the within)."

She said, "You are right. I often *begin things* and never finish them."

"I'll go home and finish something I commenced weeks ago, and I know it will be symbolic of my demonstration."

So she sewed assiduously, and the article was soon completed. Shortly after, the money came in a most curious manner.

Her husband was paid his salary twice that month. He told the people of their mistake, and they sent word to keep it.

When man asks, *believing, he must receive, for God creates His own channels!*

I have been sometimes asked, "Suppose one has several talents, how is he to know which one to choose?" Demand to be shown definitely. Say: "Infinite Spirit, give me a definite lead, reveal to me my perfect self-expression, show me which talent I am to make use of now."

I have known people to suddenly enter a new line of work, and be fully equipped, with little or no training. So make the statement: "*I am fully equipped for the Divine Plan of my life*," and be fearless in grasping opportunities.

Some people are cheerful givers, but bad receivers. They refuse gifts through pride, or some negative reason, thereby blocking their channels, and invariably find themselves eventually with little or nothing. For example: A woman who had given away a great deal of money, had a gift offered her of several thousand dollars. She refused to take it, saying she did not need it. Shortly after that, her finances were "tied up," and she found herself in debt for that amount. Man should receive gracefully the bread returning to him upon the water-freely ye have given, freely ye shall receive.

There is always the perfect balance of giving and receiving, and though man should give without thinking of returns, he violates law if he does not accept the returns which come to him; for all gifts are from God, man being merely the channel.

A thought of lack should never be held over the giver.

For example: When the man gave me the one cent, I did not say: "Poor man, he cannot afford to give me that." I saw him rich and prosperous, with his supply pouring in. It was this thought which brought it. If one has been a bad receiver, he must become a good one, and take even a postage stamp if it is given him, and open up his channels for receiving.

The Lord loveth a cheerful receiver, as well as a cheerful giver.

I have often been asked why one man is born rich and healthy, and another poor and sick.

Where there is an effect there is always a cause; there is no such thing as chance.

This question is answered through the law of reincarnation. Man goes through many births and deaths, until he knows the truth which sets him free.

He is drawn back to the earth plane through unsatisfied desire, to pay his Karmic debts, or to "fulfill his destiny."

The man born rich and healthy has had pictures in his subconscious mind, in his past life, of health and riches; and the poor and sick man, of disease and poverty. Man manifests, on any plane, the sum total of his subconscious beliefs.

However, birth and death are man-made laws, for the "wages of sin is death"; the Adamic fall in consciousness through the belief in *two powers*. The real man, spiritual man, is birthless and deathless! He never was born and has never died – "As he was in the beginning, he is now, and ever shall be!"

So through the truth, man is set free from the law of Karma, sin and death, and manifests the man made in "His image and likeness." Man's freedom comes through fulfilling his destiny, bringing into manifestation the Divine Design of his life.

His lord will say unto him: "Well done thou good and faithful servant, thou hast been faithful over a few things, I will make thee ruler over many things (death itself); enter thou into the joy of thy Lord (eternal life)."

Denials and Affirmations

"Thou shalt also decree a thing, and it shall be established unto thee."

ALL THE GOOD THAT is to be made manifest in man's life is already an accomplished fact in divine mind, and is released through man's recognition, or spoken word, so he must be careful to decree that only the Divine Idea be made manifest, for often, he decrees, through his "idle words," failure or misfortune.

It is, therefore, of the utmost importance, to word one's demands correctly, as stated in a previous chapter.

If one desires a home, friend, position or any other good thing, make the demand for the "divine selection."

For example: "Infinite Spirit, open the way for my right home, my right friend, my right position. I give thanks *it now manifests under grace in a perfect way.*"

The latter part of the statement is most important. For example: I knew a woman who demanded a thousand dollars. Her daughter was injured and they received a thousand dollars indemnity, so it did not come in a "perfect way." The demand should have been worded in this way: "Infinite Spirit, I give thanks that the one thousand dollars, which is mine by divine right, is now released, and reaches me under grace, in a perfect way."

As one grows in a financial consciousness, he should demand that the enormous sums of money, which are his by divine right, reach him under grace, in perfect ways.

It is impossible for man to release more than he thinks is possible, for one is bound by the limited expectancies of the subconscious. He must enlarge his expectancies in order to receive in a larger way.

Man so often limits himself in his demands. For example: A student made the demand for six hundred dollars, by a certain date. He did receive it, but heard afterwards, that he came very near receiving a thousand dollars, but he was given just six hundred, as the result of his spoken word.

"They limited the Holy One of Isreal." Wealth is a matter of consciousness. The French have a legend giving an example of this. A poor man was walking along a road when he met traveler, who stopped him and said: "My good friend, I see you are poor. Take this gold nugget, sell it, and you will be rich all your days."

The man was overjoyed at his good fortune, and took the nugget home. He immediately found work and became so prosperous that he did not sell the nugget. Years passed, and he became a very rich man. One day he met a poor man on the road. He stopped him and said: "My good friend, I will give you this gold nugget, which, if you sell, will make you rich for life." The mendicant took the nugget, had it valued, and found it was only brass. So we see, the first man became rich through feeling rich, thinking the nugget was gold.

Every man has within himself a gold nugget; *it is his consciousness of gold, of opulence, which brings riches into his life.* In making his demands, man begins at his *journey's end*, that is, he declares *he has already received*. "*Before* ye call I shall answer."

Continually affirming establishes the belief in the subconscious.

It would not be necessary to make an affirmation more than once if one had perfect faith! One should not plead or supplicate, but give thanks repeatedly, that he has received.

"The desert shall *rejoice* and blossom as the rose." This rejoicing which is yet in the desert (state of consciousness) opens the way for release. The Lord's Prayer is in the form of command and demand, "Give us this day our daily bread, and forgive us our debts as we forgive our debtors," and ends in praise, "For thine is the Kingdom and the Power and the Glory, forever. Amen." "Concerning the works of my hands, command ye me." So prayer is command and demand, praise and thanksgiving. The student's work is in making himself believe that "with God all things are possible."

This is easy enough to state in the abstract, but a little more difficult when confronted with a problem. For example: It was necessary for a woman to demonstrate a large sum of money within a stated time. She knew she must *do something* to get a realization (for realization is manifestation), and she demanded a "lead."

She was walking through a department store, when she saw a very beautiful pink enamel papercutter. She felt the "pull" towards it. The thought came. "I haven't a paper cutter good enough to open letters containing large cheques."

So she bought the papercutter, which the reasoning mind would have called an extravagance. When she held it in her hand, she had a flash of a picture of herself opening an envelope containing a large cheque, and in a few weeks, she received the money. The pink papercutter was her bridge of active faith.

Many stories are told of the power of the subconscious when directed in faith.

For example: A man was spending the night in a farmhouse. The windows of the room had been nailed down, and in the middle of the night he felt suffocated and made his way in the dark to the window. He could not open it, so he smashed the pane with his fist, drew in draughts of fine fresh air, and had a wonderful night's sleep.

The next morning, he found he had smashed the glass of a bookcase and the window had remained closed during the whole night. He had *supplied himself with oxygen, simply by his thought of oxygen.*

When a student starts out to demonstrate, he should never turn back. "Let not that man who wavers think that he shall receive anything of the Lord."

A colored student once made this wonderful statement, "When I asks the Father for anything, I puts my foot down, and I says: Father, I'll take nothing less than I've asked for, but more!" So man should never compromise: "Having done all – Stand." This is sometimes the most difficult time of demonstrating. The temptation comes to give up, to turn back, to compromise.

"He also serves who only stands and waits."

Demonstrations often come at the eleventh hour because man then lets go, that is, stops reasoning, and Infinite Intelligence has a chance to work.

"Man's dreary desires are answered drearily, and his impatient desires, long delayed or violently fulfilled.

For example: A woman asked me why it was she was constantly losing or breaking her glasses.

We found she often said to herself and others with vexation, "I wish I could get rid of my glasses." So her impatient desire was violently fulfilled. What she should have demanded was perfect eye-sight, but what she registered in the subconscious was simply the impatient desire to be rid of her glasses; so they were continually being broken or lost.

Two attitudes of mind cause loss: depreciation, as in the case of the woman who did not appreciate her husband, *or fear of loss*, which makes a picture of loss in the subconscious.

When a student is able to let go of his problem (cast his burden) he will have instantaneous manifestation.

For example: A woman was out during a very stormy day and her umbrella was blown inside-out. She was about to make a call on some people whom she had never met and she did not wish to make her first appearance with a dilapidated umbrella. She could not throw it away, as it did not belong to her. So in desperation, she exclaimed: "Oh, God, you take charge of this umbrella, I don't know what to do."

A moment later, a voice behind her said: "Lady, do you want your umbrella mended?" There stood an umbrella mender.

She replied, "Indeed, I do."

The man mended the umbrella, while she went into the house to pay her call, and when she returned, she had a good umbrella. So there is always an umbrella mender at hand, on man's pathway, when one puts the umbrella (or situation) in God's Hands.

One should always follow a denial with an affirmation.

For example: I was called on the 'phone late one night to treat a man whom I had never seen. He was apparently very ill. I made the statement: "I deny this appearance of disease. It is unreal, therefore cannot register in his consciousness; this man is a perfect idea in Divine Mind, pure substance expressing perfection."

There is no time or space, in Divine Mind, therefore the word reaches instantly its destination and does not "return void." I have treated patients in Europe and have found that the result was instantaneous.

I am asked so often the difference between visualizing and visioning. Visualizing is a mental process governed by the reasoning or conscious mind; visioning is a spiritual process, governed by intuition, or the super-conscious mind. The student should train his mind to receive these flashes of inspiration, and work out the "divine pictures," through definite leads. When a man can say, "I desire only that which God desires for me," his false desires fade from the consciousness, and a new set of blueprints is given him by the Master Architect, the God within. God's plan for each man transcends the limitation of the reasoning mind, and is always the square of life, containing health, wealth, love and perfect self-expression. Many a man is building for himself in imagination a bungalow when he should be building a palace.

If a student tries to force a demonstration (through the reasoning mind) he brings it to a standstill. "I will hasten it," saith the Lord. He should act only through intuition, or definite leads. "Rest in the Lord and wait patiently. Trust also in him, and he will bring it to pass."

I have seen the law work in the most astonishing manner. For example: A student stated that it was necessary for her to have a hundred dollars by the following day. It was a debt of vital importance which had to be met. I "spoke the word," declaring Spirit was "never too late" and that the supply was at hand.

That evening she phoned me of the miracle. She said that the thought came to her to go to her safe-deposit box at the bank to examine some papers. She looked over the papers, and at the bottom of the box, was a new one hundred dollar-bill. She was astounded, and said she knew she had never put it there, for she had gone through the papers many times. It may have been a materialization, as Jesus Christ materialized the loaves and fishes. Man will reach the stage where his "word is made flesh," or materialized, instantly. "The fields, ripe with the harvest," will manifest immediately, as in all of the miracles of Jesus Christ.

There is a tremendous power alone in the name Jesus Christ. It stands for *Truth Made Manifest.* He said, "Whatsoever ye ask the Father, in my name, he will give it to you."

The power of this name raises the student into the fourth dimension, where he is freed from all astral and psychic influences, and he becomes "unconditioned and absolute, as God Himself is unconditioned and absolute."

I have seen many healings accomplished by using the words, "In the name of Jesus Christ."

Christ was both person and principle; and the Christ within each man is his Redeemer and Salvation.

The Christ within, is his own fourth dimensional self, the man made in God's image and likeness. This is the self which has never failed, never known sickness or sorrow, was never born and has never died. It is the "resurrection and the life" of each man! "No man cometh to the Father save by the Son," means, that God, the Universal, working on the place of the particular, becomes the Christ in man; and the Holy Ghost, means God-in-action. So daily, man is manifesting the Trinity of Father, Son and Holy Ghost.

Man should make an art of thinking. The Master Thinker is an artist and is careful to paint only the divine designs upon the canvas of his mind; and he paints these pictures with masterly strokes of power and decision, having perfect faith that there is no power to mar their perfection and that they shall manifest in his life the ideal made real.

All power is given man (through right thinking) to bring *his heaven* upon *his earth*, and this is the *goal of the "Game of Life."*

The simple rules are fearless faith, nonresistance and love!

May each reader be now freed from that thing which has held him in bondage through the ages, standing between him and his own, and "know the Truth which makes him free" – free to fulfill his destiny, to bring into manifestation the "*Divine Design of his life*, Health, Wealth, Love and Perfect Self-Expression." "Be ye transformed by the renewing of your mind."

DENIALS AND AFFIRMATIONS

(For Prosperity)

God is my unfailing supply, and large sums of money come to me quickly, under grace, in perfect ways.

(For Right Conditions)

Every plan my Father in heaven has not planned, shall be dissolved and dissipated, and the Divine Idea now comes to pass.

(For Right Conditions)

Only that which is true of God is true of me, for I and the Father are ONE.

(For Faith)

As I am one with God, I am one with my good, for God is both the *Giver* and the *Gift*. I cannot separate the *Giver* from the gift.

(For Right Conditions)

Divine Love now dissolves and dissipates every wrong condition in my mind, body and affairs. Divine Love is the most powerful chemical in the universe, and *dissolves everything* which is not of itself!

(For Health)

Divine Love floods my consciousness with health, and every cell in my body is filled with light.

(For the Eyesight)

My eyes are God's eyes, I see with the eyes of spirit. I see clearly the open way; there are no obstacles on my pathway. I see clearly the perfect plan.

(For Guidance)

I am divinely sensitive to my intuitive leads, and give instant obedience to Thy will.

(For the Hearing)

My ears are God's ears, I hear with the ears of spirit. I am nonresistant and am willing to be led. I hear glad tidings of great joy.

(For Right Work)

I have a perfect work
In a perfect way;
I give a perfect service
For perfect pay.

(For Freedom from all Bondage)

I cast this burden on the Christ within, and I go free!

Your Word is Your Wand

Affirmations of Truth

Your Word is Your Wand

Man's word is his wand filled with magic and power!

Jesus Christ emphasized the power of the word; "By thy words thou shalt be justified and by thy words thou shalt be condemned," and "death and life are in power of the tongue."

So man has power to change an unhappy condition by waving over it the wand of his word.

In the place of sorrow appears joy, in the place of sickness appears health, in the place of lack appears plenty.

For example: A woman came for a treatment for prosperity. She possessed just two dollars in the world.

I said: "We bless the two dollars and know that you have the magic purse of the Spirit; it can never be depleted; as money goes out, immediately money comes in, under grace in perfect ways.

I see it always crammed, jammed with money: yellow bills, green bills, pink checks, blue checks, white checks, gold, silver and currency. I see it bulging with abundance!"

She replied: "I feel my bag heavy with money," and was so filled with faith that she gave me one of her dollars as a love offering. I did not dare refuse it and see lack for her, as it was important that I hold the picture of plenty.

Shortly afterwards she was made a gift of six thousand dollars. Fearless faith and the spoken word brought it to pass.

The affirmation of the magic purse is very powerful, as it brings a vivid picture to the mind. It is impossible not to see your purse or wallet filled with money when using the words, "crammed, jammed."

The imaging faculty is the creative faculty and it is important to choose words which bring a flash of the fulfillment of the demand.

Never force a picture by visualizing; let the Divine Idea flash into your conscious mind; then the student is working according to the Divine Design.

(See *The Game of Life and How to Play It*)

Jesus Christ said: "Ye shall know the Truth and the Truth shall make you free."

This means that man must know the Truth of every situation which confronts him.

There is no Truth in lack or limitation. *He waves over it the wand of His Word and the wilderness rejoices and blossoms as the rose.*

Fear, doubt, anxiety, anger, resentment pull down the cells of the body, shock the nervous system and are the causes of disease and disaster.

Happiness and health must be earned by absolute control of the emotional nature.

Power moves but is never moved. When man stands calm and serene, has a good appetite, feels contented and happy when appearances are against him, he has reached mastery. Then he has power to "rebuke the winds and the waves," to control conditions.

His word is his wand and he transmutes apparent failure into success.

He knows his universal supply is endless and immediate and all his needs manifest instantly on the external.

For example, a woman at sea awoke in the morning hearing the foghorns blowing. A dense fog had settled on the ocean with no apparent signs of clearing. She immediately spoke the word: "There are no fogs in Divine Mind, so let the fog be lifted! I give thanks for the sun!"

Soon the sun came out, for man has dominion over "the elements – over all created things."

Every man has power to lift the fog in his life. It may be a fog of lack of money, love, happiness or health.

Give thanks for the sun!

Success Affirmations

SUCCESS

THERE ARE CERTAIN words or pictures which impress the subconscious mind.

For example: A man called asking me to speak the word for his right work.

I gave him the statement: "Behold I have set before thee the open door of destiny and no man shall shut it!"

It didn't seem to make much impression, so I was inspired to add: "And no man shall shut it for it is *nailed back!*"

The man was electrified and went out walking on air. Within a few weeks he was called to a distant city to fill a wonderful position which came about in a miraculous way.

I give another example of a woman who fearlessly followed a "hunch."

She was working for a small salary when she read my book, *The Game of Life and How to Play It.* The thought came in a flash, to start in business for herself and open a Tearoom and Candy Shop.

The idea staggered her at first, but it persisted, so she boldly went forth and procured a shop and assistants.

She "spoke the word for supply," for she did not have money to back her enterprise. It came in miraculous ways, and the shop opened!

From the first day it was filled with people, and now it is "crammed jammed"; they stand in line and wait.

One day, being a holiday, her assistants became gloomy and said they could not expect to do much business. My student, however, replied that God was her supply and every day was a good day.

In the afternoon an old friend came in to see the shop and bought a two pound box of candy. He gave her a check and when she looked at it she found it was for a hundred dollars. So it was indeed a good day! One hundred dollars for a box of candy!

She says every morning she enters the shop with wonder and gives thanks that she had the fearless faith that wins!

AFFIRMATIONS

THE DECKS ARE NOW cleared for Divine Action and my own comes to me under grace in a magical way.

* * * * *

I now let go of worn-out conditions and worn-out things.
Divine order is established in my mind, body and affairs.
"Behold, I make all things new."

* * * * *

My seeming impossible good now comes to pass, the unexpected now happens!

* * * * *

The "four winds of success" now blow to me my own.
From North, South, East and West comes my endless good.

* * * * *

The Christ in me is risen, I now fulfill my destiny.

* * * * *

Endless good now comes to me in endless ways.

* * * * *

I clap my cymbals and rejoice, for Jehovah goes before me making clear, easy and successful my way!

* * * * *

I give thanks for my whirlwind success.

I sweep all before me for I work with the Spirit and follow the Divine Plan of my life.

* * * * *

My Spiritual Sporting blood is up! I am more than equal to this situation.

* * * * *

I am awake to my good, and gather in the harvest of endless opportunities.

* * * * *

I am harmonious, poised and magnetic.
I now draw to myself *my own*. My power is God's power and is irresistible!

* * * * *

Divine order is now established in my mind, body and affairs.
I see clearly and act quickly and my greatest expectations come to pass in a miraculous way.

* * * * *

There is no competition on the Spiritual plane. What is rightfully mine *is given me under grace*.

* * * * *

I have within me an undiscovered country, which is revealed to me now, in the name of Jesus Christ.

* * * * *

Behold! I have set before thee the open door of Destiny and no man shall shut it, for it is *nailed back*.

* * * * *

The tide of Destiny has turned and everything comes my way.

* * * * *

I banish the past and now live in the wonderful now, where happy surprises come to me each day.

* * * * *

There are no lost opportunities in Divine Mind, as one door shut *another door opened*.

* * * * *

I have a magical work in a magical way, I give magical service for magical pay.

* * * * *

The genius within me is now released. I now fulfill my destiny.

* * * * *

I make friends with hindrances and every obstacle becomes a stepping-stone. Every-thing in the Universe, visible and invisible, is working to bring to me my own.

* * * * *

I give thanks that the walls of Jericho fall down and all lack, limitation and failure are wiped out of my consciousness in the name of Jesus Christ.

* * * * *

I am now on the royal road of Success, Happiness and Abundance, all the traffic goes my way.

* * * * *

I will not weary of well-doing, for when I least expect it I shall reap.

* * * * *

Jehovah goes before me and the battle is won!

All enemy thoughts are wiped out.
I am victorious in the name of Jesus Christ.

* * * * *

There are no obstacles in Divine Mind, therefore, there is nothing to obstruct my good.

* * * * *

All obstacles now vanish from my pathway.
Doors fly open, gates are lifted and I enter the Kingdom of fulfillment, under grace.

* * * * *

Rhythm, harmony and balance are now established in my mind, body and affairs.

* * * * *

New fields of Divine activity now open for me and these fields are white with the harvest.

* * * * *

Man's will is powerless to interfere with God's will. God's will is now done in my mind, body and affairs.

* * * * *

God's plan for me is permanent and cannot be budged.
I am true to my *heavenly vision*.

* * * * *

"The Divine Plan of my life now takes shape in definite, concrete experiences leading to my heart's desire."

* * * * *

I now draw from the Universal Substance, with irresistible power and determination, that which is mine by Divine Right.

* * * * *

I do not resist this situation. I put it in the hands of Infinite Love and Wisdom. *Let the Divine idea now come to pass.*

* * * * *

My good now flows to me in a steady, unbroken, ever-increasing stream of success, happiness and abundance.

* * * * *

There are no lost opportunities in the Kingdom.
As one door shuts another door opens.

* * * * *

"There is nothing to fear for there is no power to hurt."
I walk up to the lion on my pathway and find an angel in armor, and victory in the name of Jesus Christ.

* * * * *

I am in perfect harmony with the working of the law. I stand aside and let Infinite Intelligence make easy and successful my way.

* * * * *

The ground I am on is holy ground; The ground I am on is successful ground.

* * * * *

New fields of Divine Activity now open for me.
Unexpected doors fly open, unexpected channels are free.

* * * * *

What God has done for others He can do for me and more!

* * * * *

I am as necessary to God as He is to me, for I *am* the channel to bring *His plan to pass*.

* * * * *

I do not limit God by seeing limitation in myself. With God and myself all things are possible.

* * * * *

Giving precedes receiving and my gifts to others precede God's gifts to me.

* * * * *

Every man is a golden link in the chain of my good.

* * * * *

My poise is built upon a rock. I see clearly and act quickly.

* * * * *

God cannot fail, so I cannot fail. "The warrior within me" has already won.

* * * * *

Thy Kingdom come in me, Thy will be done in me and my affairs.

Prosperity Affirmations

PROSPERITY

(See also *The Game of Life and How to Play It*.)

Man comes into the world financed by God, with all that he desires or requires already on his pathway.

This supply is released through faith and the *Spoken Word*.

"If thou canst believe, all things are possible."

For example: A woman came to me one day, to tell me of her experience in using an affirmation she had read in my book, *The Game of Life and How to Play It*.

She was without experience but desired a good position on the stage. She took the affirmation: "Infinite Spirit, open the way for my great abundance. I am an irresistible magnet for all that belongs to me by Divine Right."

She was given a very important part in a successful opera.

She said: "It was a miracle, due to that affirmation, which I repeated hundreds of times."

AFFIRMATIONS

I NOW DRAW FROM the abundance of the spheres my immediate and endless supply.

All channels are free!

All doors are open!

* * * * *

I now release the gold-mine within me. I am linked with an endless golden stream of prosperity which comes to me under grace in perfect ways.

* * * * *

Goodness and mercy shall follow me all the days of my life and I shall dwell in the house of abundance forever.

* * * * *

My God is a God of plenty and I now receive all that I desire or require, and more.

* * * * *

All that is mine by Divine Right is now released and reaches me in great avalanches of abundance, under grace in miraculous ways.

* * * * *

My supply is endless, inexhaustible and immediate and comes to me under grace in perfect ways.

* * * * *

All channels are free and all doors fly open for my immediate and endless, Divinely Designed supply.
My ships come in over a calm sea, under grace in perfect ways.

* * * * *

I give thanks that the millions which are mine by Divine Right, now pour in and pile up under grace in perfect ways.

* * * * *

Unexpected doors fly open, unexpected channels are free, and endless avalanches of abundance are poured out upon me, under grace in perfect ways.

* * * * *

I spend money under direct inspiration wisely and fearlessly, knowing my supply is endless and immediate.

* * * * *

I am fearless in letting money go out, knowing God is my immediate and endless supply.

Happiness Affirmations

HAPPINESS

IN THAT WONDERFUL moving picture, "The Thief of Bagdad," we were told in letters of light that *happiness must be earned!*

It is earned through perfect control of the emotional nature.

There can be no happiness where there is fear, apprehension or dread. With *perfect faith in God* comes a feeling of *security* and *happiness*.

When man *knows* that there is an invincible power that protects him and all that he loves, and brings to him every righteous desire of the heart, he relaxes all nervous tension and is happy and satisfied.

He is undisturbed by adverse appearances, knowing that *Infinite Intelligence* is protecting his interests and utilizing every situation to bring his good to pass.

"I will make a way in the wilderness and rivers in a desert."

Uneasy lies the head that wears a frown. Anger, resentment, ill-will, jealousy and revenge rob man of his happiness and bring sickness, failure and poverty in their wake.

Resentment has ruined more homes than drink and killed more people than war.

For example: There was a woman who was healthy and happy and married to a man she loved.

The man died and left part of his estate to a relative. The woman was filled with resentment. She lost weight, was unable to do her work, developed gall-stones and became very ill.

A metaphysician called upon her one day. He said: "Woman, see what hate and resentment have done to you; they have caused hard stones to form in your body and only forgiveness and good-will can cure you."

The woman saw the Truth of the statement. She became harmonious and forgiving and regained her splendid health.

AFFIRMATIONS

I AM NOW DELUGED with the happiness that was planned for me in the Beginning.

My barns are full, my cup flows over with joy.

* * * * *

My endless good now comes to me in endless ways.

* * * * *

I have a wonderful joy in a wonderful way, and my wonderful joy has come to stay.

* * * * *

Happy surprises come to me each day. "I look with wonder at that which is before me."

* * * * *

I walk boldly up to the lion on my pathway and find it is a friendly airedale.

* * * * *

I am harmonious, happy, radiant; detached from the tyranny of fear.

* * * * *

My happiness is built upon a rock. It is mine now and for all eternity.

* * * * *

My good now flows to me in a steady unbroken, ever-increasing stream of happiness.

* * * * *

My happiness is God's affair, therefore, no one can interfere.

* * * * *

As I am one with God I am now one with my heart's desire.

* * * * *

I give thanks for my permanent happiness, my permanent health, my permanent wealth, my permanent love.

* * * * *

I am harmonious, happy and Divinely magnetic, and now draw to me my ships over a calm sea.

* * * * *

God's ideas for me are perfect and permanent.

* * * * *

My heart's desire is a perfect idea in Divine Mind, incorruptible and indestructible, and now comes to pass, under grace in a magical way.

Love Affirmations

LOVE

With love usually comes terrific fear. Nearly every woman comes into the world with a mythical woman in the back of her mind who is to rob her of her love.

She has been called "the other woman." Of course it comes from woman's belief in duality. So long as she visualizes interference, it will come.

It is usually very difficult for a woman to see herself loved by the man she loves, so these affirmations are to impress the truth of the situation upon her subconscious mind, for in reality there is *only oneness*.

(See *The Game of Life and How to Play It*.)

AFFIRMATIONS

As I am one with God, the Undivided One, I am one with my undivided love and undivided happiness.

* * * * *

The Light of the Christ within now wipes out all fear, doubt, anger and resentment. God's love pours through me, an irresistible magnetic current. I see only perfection and draw to me my own.

* * * * *

Divine Love, through me, now dissolves all seeming obstacles and makes clear, easy and successful my way.

* * * * *

I love everyone and everyone loves me. My apparent enemy becomes my friend, a golden link in the chain of my good.

* * * * *

I am at peace with myself and with the whole world. I love everyone and everyone loves me.
The flood gates of my good now open.

Marriage Affirmations

MARRIAGE

Unless marriage is built upon the rock of *oneness* it cannot stand; "Two souls with but a single thought, two hearts that beat as one."

The poet understood this, for unless man and wife are living the same thoughts (or living in the same thought world), they must inevitably drift apart.

Thought is a tremendous vibratory force and man is drawn to his thought creations.

For example: A man and woman married and were apparently happy. The man became successful and his tastes improved, but the wife still lived in a limited consciousness.

Whenever the man bought anything he went to the best shops and selected what he needed regardless of price.

Whenever the wife went out she haunted the Five and Ten Cent Stores.

He was living (in thought), on Fifth Avenue and her thought world was on Third Avenue.

Eventually the break and separation came.

We see this so often in the cases of rich and successful men who desert their faithful, hardworking wives later in life.

The wife must keep pace with her husband's taste and ambitions and live in his thought world, for *where* a man thinketh in his heart *there is he*.

There is for each person his "other half" or divine selection.

These two are one in their thought worlds. These are the two "whom God has joined together and no man shall (or can) part asunder." "The twain shall be made one," for in the superconscious mind of each is the same Divine Plan.

AFFIRMATION

I GIVE THANKS that the marriage made in heaven is now made manifest upon earth.

"The twain shall be made one" now and for all eternity.

Forgiveness Affirmations

FORGIVENESS

* * * * *

AFFIRMATIONS

I FORGIVE EVERYONE and everyone forgives me. The gates swing open for my good.

* * * * *

I call on the law of forgiveness. I am free from mistakes and the consequences of mistakes. I am under grace and not under karmic law.

* * * * *

Though my mistakes be as scarlet, I shall be washed whiter than snow.

* * * * *

What didn't happen in the Kingdom never happened anywhere.

Words of Wisdom Affirmations

WORDS OF WISDOM

* * * * *

AFFIRMATIONS

"Faith without nerve is dead."

* * * * *

There is never a slip 'twixt the right cup and the right lip.

* * * * *

Never look or you'd never leap.

* * * * *

God works in unexpected places, through unexpected people, at unexpected times, His wonders to perform.

* * * * *

Power moves but is never moved.

* * * * *

Loving your neighbor means not to limit your neighbor in word, thought or deed.

* * * * *

"Never argue with a hunch."

* * * * *

Christopher Columbus followed a hunch.

* * * * *

The Kingdom of Heaven is the realm of perfect ideas.

* * * * *

It is dark before the dawn but the dawn never fails. Trust in the dawn.

* * * * *

When in doubt play trumps, *do the fearless thing*.

* * * * *

It is the fearless things that count.

* * * * *

Never do today what intuition says to do tomorrow.

* * * * *

It's a great life if you don't reason.

* * * * *

Regard your neighbor as yourself.

* * * * *

Never hinder another's hunch.

* * * * *

Selfishness binds and blocks. Every loving and unselfish thought has in it the germ of success.

* * * * *

Be not weary of make-believing. When you least expect it you shall reap.

* * * * *

Faith is elastic. Stretch it to the end of your demonstration.

* * * * *

Before you call you are answered, for the supply precedes the demand.

* * * * *

What you do for others you are doing for yourself.

* * * * *

Every act committed while angry or resentful brings unhappy reaction.

* * * * *

Sorrow and disappointment follow in the wake of deceit and subterfuge. The way of the transgressor is hard. "No good thing will be withheld from him who *walks uprightly*."

* * * * *

There is no power in evil. It is nothing; therefore can only come to nothing.

* * * * *

Fear and impatience demagnetize. Poise magnetizes.

* * * * *

Drown the reasoning mind with your affirmation. Jehoshaphat clapped his cymbals so that he wouldn't hear himself think.

* * * * *

All bondage is an illusion of the race consciousness. There is always a way out of every situation, under grace. Every man is free to do the will of God.

* * * * *

Sure-ism is stronger than Optimism.

* * * * *

"Divine ideas never conflict."

* * * * *

It is dangerous to stop in the middle of a *hunch*.
Infinite Spirit is never too late.

Faith Affirmations

FAITH

Hope looks forward, *Faith knows it has already received and acts accordingly.*

In my classes I often emphasize the importance of digging ditches (or preparing for the thing asked for) which shows active faith and brings the demonstration to pass.

(See *The Game of Life and How to Play It*.)

A man in my class, whom I called "the life of the party," because he always tried to find a question I couldn't answer, but he never succeeded, asked: "Why is it then, a lot of women who prepare Hope Chests never get married?" I replied: "Because it is a Hope Chest and not a *Faith Chest*."

The prospective bride also violates law in telling others about it. Her friends come in and sit on the Hope Chest and either doubt or hope she'll never succeed.

"Pray to thy Father which is in secret, and thy Father which seeth in secret shall reward thee openly."

The student should never talk of a demonstration until it "has jelled," or comes to pass on the external.

So a Hope Chest should become a Faith Chest and be kept from the public eye, and the word spoken for the Divine Selection of a husband, under grace in a perfect way.

Those whom God hath joined together no thought can put asunder.

AFFIRMATIONS

Adverse appearances work for my good, for God utilizes every person and every situation to bring to me my heart's desire.

"Hindrances are friendly" and obstacles spring boards!
I now jump into my good!

* * * * *

As I am one with the *Undivided One*, I am one with my undivided good.

* * * * *

As the needle in the compass is true to the north, what is rightfully mine is true to me.
I am the North!

* * * * *

"I am now linked by an invisible, unbreakable magnetic cord with all that belongs to me by Divine Right!

* * * * *

Thy Kingdom is come, Thy will is done in me and my affairs.

* * * * *

Every plan my Father in heaven has not planned is dissolved and obliterated and the Divine Design of my life now comes to pass.

* * * * *

What God has given me can never be taken from me for His gifts are for all eternity.

* * * * *

My faith is built upon a rock and my heart's desire now comes to pass, under grace in a miraculous way.

* * * * *

I see my good in a golden glow of glory. I see my fields shining white with the harvest.

* * * * *

God is my unfailing and immediate supply of all good.

* * * * *

I am poised and powerful, my greatest expectations are realized in a miraculous way.

* * * * *

I water my wilderness with faith and suddenly it blossoms as the rose.

* * * * *

I now exercise my fearless faith in three ways – by thinking, speaking and acting.
I am unmoved by appearances, therefore appearances move.

* * * * *

I stand steadfast, immovable, giving thanks for my seeming impossible good to come to pass, for I know, with God, it is easy of accomplishment, and His time is *now*.

* * * * *

God's plans for me are built upon a rock. What was mine in the beginning, is mine now and ever shall be mine.

* * * * *

I *know* there is nothing to defeat God, therefore, there is nothing to defeat me.

* * * * *

I wait patiently on the Lord, I trust in Him, I fret not myself because of evil doers (for every man is a golden link in the chain of my good) and He now gives to me the desires of my heart! (See 37th Psalm.)

* * * * *

I have now the fearless faith of the Christ within. At my approach barriers vanish and obstacles disappear.

* * * * *

I am steadfast, immovable, for the fields are already white with the harvest. My fearless faith in God now brings the Divine Design of my life to pass.

* * * * *

All fear is now banished in the name of Jesus Christ, for I know there is no power to hurt.
God is the one and only power.

* * * * *

I am in perfect harmony with the working of the law, for I know that Infinite Intelligence knows nothing of obstacles, time or space. It knows only completion.

* * * * *

God works in unexpected and magic ways His wonders to perform.

* * * * *

I now prepare for the fulfillment of my heart's desire. I show God I believe His promise will be kept.

* * * * *

I now dig my ditches deep with faith and understanding and my heart's desire comes to pass in a surprising way.

* * * * *

My ditches will be filled at the right time, bringing all that I have asked for, and more!

* * * * *

I now "put to flight the army of the aliens" (negative thoughts). They feed on fear and starve on faith.

* * * * *

God's ideas cannot be moved, therefore, what is mine by Divine Right will always be with me.

* * * * *

I give thanks that I now receive the righteous desires of my heart.
Mountains are removed, valleys exalted and every crooked place made straight.
I am in the Kingdom of fulfillment.

* * * * *

I have perfect confidence in God and God has perfect confidence in me.

* * * * *

God's promises are built upon a rock. As I have asked I *must* receive.

* * * * *

"Let me never wander from my heart's desire."

* * * * *

I do not limit the Holy One of Israel, in word, thought or deed. With God all things are easy and possible now.

* * * * *

I now stand aside and watch God work.

It interests me to see how quickly and easily He brings the desires of my heart to pass.

* * * * *

Before I called I was answered and I now gather in my harvest in a remarkable way.

* * * * *

He who watches over my heart's desire "Neither slumbers nor sleeps."

* * * * *

Seeming impossible doors now open, seeming impossible channels are free, in the name of *Jesus Christ*.

* * * * *

My good is a perfect and permanent idea in Divine Mind, and must manifest for there is nothing to prevent.

* * * * *

I cast every burden on the Christ within and I go free!
(See *The Game of Life and How to Play It*.)

Loss Affirmations

LOSS

If man loses anything it shows there is a belief of loss in his subconscious mind. As he erases this false belief, the article, or its equivalent will appear on the external.

For example: A woman lost a silver pencil in a theatre. She made every effort to find it but it was not returned.

She denied loss, taking the affirmation: "I deny loss, there is no loss in Divine Mind, therefore I cannot lose that pencil. I will receive it or its equivalent."

Several weeks elapsed. One day she was with a friend who wore about her neck on a cord, a beautiful gold pencil, who turned to her and said: "Do you want this pencil? I paid fifty dollars for it at Tiffany's."

The woman was aghast, and replied (almost forgetting to thank her friend) "Oh! God aren't you wonderful! The silver pencil wasn't good enough for me!"

Man can only lose what doesn't belong to him by Divine Right, or isn't good enough for him.

AFFIRMATIONS

There is no loss in Divine Mind, therefore, I cannot lose anything that is rightfully mine.

Infinite Intelligence is never too late! Infinite Intelligence knows the way of recovery.

* * * * *

There is no loss in Divine Mind, therefore, I cannot lose anything which belongs to me.

It will be restored or I receive its equivalent.

Debt Affirmations

DEBT

IF A MAN IS in debt or people owe him money, it shows that a belief of debt is in his subconscious mind.

This belief must be neutralized in order to change conditions.

For example: A woman came to me saying a man had owed her a thousand dollars for years which she could not compel him to pay.

I said: "You must work on yourself, not the man," and gave her this statement: "I deny debt, there is no debt in Divine Mind, no man owes me anything, all is squared. I send that man love and forgiveness."

In a few weeks she received a letter from him saying he intended sending the money and in about a month came the thousand dollars.

If the student owes money, change the statement: "There is no debt in Divine Mind, therefore, I owe no man anything, all is *squared*.

All my obligations are now wiped out, under grace in a perfect way."

AFFIRMATIONS

I deny debt, there is no debt in Divine Mind, therefore, I owe no man anything.

All obligations are now wiped out under grace in a miraculous way.

* * * * *

I deny debt, there is no debt in Divine Mind, no man owes me anything, all is squared. I send forth love and forgiveness.

Sales Affirmations

SALES

A WOMAN WHO LIVED in a country town wished to sell her house and furniture. It was in the winter with snow so deep it was almost impossible for cars or wagons to reach her door.

As she had asked God to sell her furniture to the right person for the right price she was unmindful of appearances.

She polished the furniture, pushed it into the middle of the room and prepared to sell it.

She said: "I never looked out of the window at the blizzard, I simply trusted God's promises."

In miraculous ways people drove up and all the furniture was sold, and the house also, without paying any commission to an agent.

Faith never looks out of the window at the blizzard, it simply prepares for the blessing asked for.

AFFIRMATION

I give thanks that this article (or property) is now sold to the right person or persons for the right price, giving perfect satisfaction.

Interviews Affirmations

INTERVIEWS

* * * * *

AFFIRMATIONS

There is no competition on the Spiritual plane. What is mine is given me, under grace.

* * * * *

I am identified in love with the Spirit of this person (or persons). God protects my interests and the Divine Idea now comes out of this situation.

Guidance Affirmations

GUIDANCE

Always on man's pathway is his message or his lead.

For example: A woman was much troubled over an unhappy situation. She thought to herself, "Will it ever clear up?"

Her maid was standing near and commenced to tell her of her experiences. The woman was too worried to be interested but listened patiently. The maid was saying: "I worked in a hotel once where there was a very amusing gardener, he always said such funny things. It had been raining for three days and I said to him: 'Do you think it will ever clear up?' And he replied, 'My God, doesn't it always clear up?'"

The woman was amazed! It was the answer to her thoughts. She said reverently, "Yes, with my God it always clears up!" Soon after, her problem did clear up in an unexpected way.

* * * * *

AFFIRMATIONS

Infinite Spirit, give me wisdom to make the most of my opportunities. Never let me miss a trick.

* * * * *

I am always under direct inspiration. I know just what to do and give instant obedience to my intuitive leads.

* * * * *

My angel of destiny goes before me, keeping me in the Way.

* * * * *

All power is given unto me to be meek and lowly of heart.
I am willing to come last, therefore, I come first!

* * * * *

I now place my personal will upon the altar.
Your will, not my will; Your way not my way; Your time not my time — *and in the twinkling of an eye it is done!*

* * * * *

There are no mysteries in the Kingdom. Whatever I should know will now be revealed to me, under grace.

* * * * *

I am a perfect non-resistant instrument for God to work through, and His perfect plan for me now comes to pass in a magic way.

Protection Affirmations

PROTECTION

* * * * *

AFFIRMATIONS

I AM SURROUNDED by the White Light of the Christ, through which nothing negative can penetrate.

* * * * *

I walk in the Light of the Christ and my fear giants dwindle into nothingness.
There is nothing to oppose my good.

Memory Affirmation

MEMORY

* * * * *

AFFIRMATION

THERE IS NO LOSS of memory in Divine Mind, therefore, I recollect everything I should remember and I forget all that is not for my good.

The Divine Design Affirmations

THE DIVINE DESIGN

(*See also The Game of Life and How to Play It.*)

THERE IS A DIVINE Design for each man!

Just as the perfect picture of the oak is in the acorn, the divine pattern of his life is in the super-conscious mind of man.

In the Divine Design there is no limitation, only health, wealth, love and perfect self-expression.

So on man's pathway there is always a Divine Selection. Each day he must live according to the Divine Plan or have unhappy reactions.

For example: A woman moved into a new apartment which she had almost furnished, when the thought came to her: "On that side of the room should stand a Chinese cabinet!

Not long after, she was walking by an antique shop. She glanced in and there stood a magnificent Chinese cabinet about eight feet high, elaborately carved.

She entered and asked the price. The salesman said it was worth a thousand dollars but the woman who owned it was willing to take less. The man added: "What will you offer for it?" The woman paused and the price "Two hundred dollars" came into her mind, so she answered: "Two hundred dollars." The man said he would let her know if the offer were satisfactory.

She did not want to cheat anyone or get anything which was not rightfully hers, so going home she said repeatedly: "*If it's mine I can't lose it and of it isn't mine, I don't want it.*" It was a snowy day and she said she emphasized her words by kicking the snow from right to left, clearing a pathway to her apartment.

Several days elapsed when she was notified that the woman was willing to sell the cabinet for two hundred dollars.

There is a supply for every demand, from Chinese cabinets to millions of dollars.

"Before ye call I shall answer," but, unless it is the Divinely Selected cabinet or millions they would never bring happiness.

"Except the Lord build the house, they labor in vain that build it." (Psalm 127-1.)

* * * * *

AFFIRMATIONS

I LET GO OF EVERYTHING not divinely designed for me, and the perfect plan of my life now comes to pass.

* * * * *

What is mine by Divine Right can never be taken from me.
God's perfect plan for me is built upon a rock.

* * * * *

I follow the magic path of intuition and find myself in my Promised Land, under grace.

* * * * *

My mind, body and affairs are now molded according to the Divine pattern within.

* * * * *

"God is the only power and that power is within me. There is only one plan, God's plan, and that plan now comes to pass."

* * * * *

"I give thanks that I now bring forth from the Universal Substance everything that satisfies all the righteous desires of my heart."

* * * * *

The divine Design of my life now comes to pass. I now fill the place that I can fill and no one else can fill. I now do the things which I can do and no one else can do.

* * * * *

I am fully equipped for the Divine Plan of my life; I am more than equal to the situation.

* * * * *

All doors now open for happy surprises and the Divine Plan of my life is speeded up under grace.

Health Affirmations

HEALTH

When man is harmonious and happy he is healthy! All sickness comes from sin or violation of Spiritual Law.

Jesus Christ said: "Be thou healed, your sins are forgiven."

Resentment, ill-will, hate, fear, etc., etc., tear down the cells of the body and poison the blood. (See *The Game of Life and How to Play It*.)

Accidents, old age and death itself, come from holding wrong mental pictures.

When man sees himself as God sees him, he will become a radiant being, timeless, birthless and deathless, for "God made man in His likeness and in His image."

* * * * *

AFFIRMATIONS

I deny fatigue, for there is nothing to tire me. I live in the Kingdom of eternal joy and absorbing interests.

My body is "the body electric," timeless and tireless, birthless and deathless.

Time and space are obliterated!

* * * * *

I live in the wonderful now, birthless and deathless!
I am one with *The One!*

* * * * *

Thou in me art:

Eternal joy.
Eternal youth.
Eternal wealth.
Eternal health.
Eternal love.
Eternal life.

* * * * *

I am a Spiritual Being – my body is perfect, made in His likeness and image.
The Light of the Christ now streams through every cell. I give thanks for my radiant health.

Eyes Affirmations

EYES

(Imperfect vision. Correspondences – Fear, suspicion, seeing obstacles. Watching for unhappy events to come to pass – living in the past or future – not living in the NOW.)

* * * * *

AFFIRMATIONS

The Light of the Christ now floods my eyeballs. I have the crystal clear vision of the Spirit. I see clearly and distinctly there are no obstacles on my pathway. I see clearly the fulfillment of my heart's desire.

* * * * *

I have the X-ray eye of the Spirit. I see through apparent obstacles. I see clearly the miracle come to pass.

* * * * *

I have the crystal clear vision of the Spirit, I see clearly the open road. There are no obstacles on my pathway. I now see miracles and wonders come to pass.

* * * * *

I give thanks for my perfect sight. I see God in every face, I see good in every situation.

* * * * *

I have the crystal clear vision of the Spirit. I look up and down and all around, for my good comes from North, South, East and West.

* * * * *

My eyes are God's eyes, perfect and flawless. The Light of the Christ floods my eyeballs and streams on my pathway. I see clearly there are no lions on my way, only angels and endless blessings.

Anemia Affirmation

ANEMIA

(*Correspondence – Unfed desires – lack of happiness.*)

* * * * *

AFFIRMATION

I AM NOURISHED by the Spirit within. Every cell in my body is filled with light. I give thanks for radiant health and endless happiness. (*This statement may be used in the healing of any disease.*)

Ears Affirmations

EARS

(*Deafness – Correspondence – Strong personal will, stubbornness and a desire not to hear certain things.*)

* * * * *

AFFIRMATION

MY EARS ARE THE ears of Spirit. The Light of the Christ now streams through my ears dissolving all hardness or malformation.

I hear clearly the voice of intuition and give instant obedience.

I hear clearly glad tidings of great joy.

Rheumatism Affirmations

RHEUMATISM

(*Correspondence – Fault finding, criticism, etc.*)

* * * * *

AFFIRMATION

THE LIGHT OF THE Christ now floods my consciousness dissolving all acid thoughts.
   I love everyone and everyone loves me.
   I give thanks for my radiant health and happiness.

False Growths Affirmations

FALSE GROWTHS

(*Correspondence – Jealousy, hatred, resentment, fear, etc., etc.*)

* * * * *

AFFIRMATION

EVERY PLANT MY FATHER in Heaven has not planted shall be rooted up. All false ideas in my consciousness are now obliterated. The Light of the Christ streams through every cell and I give thanks for my radiant health and happiness now and forevermore.

Heart Disease Affirmations

HEART DISEASE

(*Correspondence – Fear, Anger, etc.*)

* * * * *

AFFIRMATION

My heart is a perfect idea in Divine Mind and is now in its right place, doing its right work.

It is a happy heart, a fearless heart and a loving heart.

The Light of the Christ streams through every cell and I give thanks for my radiant health.

Animal Affirmations

ANIMALS

(*Dog: for example*)

* * * * *

AFFIRMATIONS

I DENY ANY APPEARANCE of disorder. This dog is a perfect idea in Divine Mind and now expresses God's perfect Idea of a perfect dog.

* * * * *

Infinite Intelligence illumines and directs this animal. It is a perfect idea in Divine Mind and is always in its right place.

Elements Affirmations

THE ELEMENTS

MAN IS MADE IN God's likeness and image (Imagination) and is given power and dominion over all created things.

He has power to "rebuke the winds and the waves," check floods or bring rain when it is needed.

There is a tribe of American Indians who live in the desert country and depend on the power of prayer only, to bring rain to water their crops.

They have a rain dance, which is a form of prayer, but no chief is allowed to take part who has any fear.

They give exhibitions of courage before they are admitted to the ceremonies.

A woman, who was an eye-witness, told me that out of a blue sky came *a deluge of rain; the sun still shining.*

FIRE AFFIRMATION

FIRE IS MAN'S FRIEND and is always in its right place doing its right work.

* * * * *

DROUGHT AFFIRMATION

THERE IS NO DROUGHT in Divine Mind. I give thanks for the right amount of rain to nourish these crops or garden.

I see clearly this gentle downpour and the manifestation is *now.*

* * * * *

STORMS AFFIRMATION

THE CHRIST WITHIN now rebukes the winds and the waves and there comes a great calm.

I see clearly peace established on land and sea.

Journey Affirmation

JOURNEY AFFIRMATION

I GIVE THANKS for the Divinely planned journey under Divinely planned conditions with the Divinely planned supply.

Miscellaneous

MISCELLANEOUS

THE THING YOU DISLIKE or hate will surely come upon you, for when man hates, he makes a vivid picture in the subconscious mind and it objectifies.

The only way to erase these pictures is through non-resistance.

(See *The Game of Life and How to Play It*.)

For example: A woman was interested in a man who told her repeatedly of his charming women cousins.

She was jealous and resentful and he passed out of her life.

Later on she met another man to whom she was much attracted. In the course of their conversation he mentioned some women cousins he was very fond of.

She resented it, then laughed, for here were her old friends "the cousins" back again.

This time she tried non-resistance. She blessed all the cousins in the Universe and sent them good-will, for she knew if she didn't, every man she met would be stocked up with women relations.

It was successful for she never heard cousins mentioned again.

This is the reason so many people have unhappy experiences repeated in their lives.

I knew a woman who bragged of her troubles. She would go about saying to people; "I know what trouble is!" and then wait for their words of sympathy.

Of course, the more she mentioned her troubles, the more she had, for by her words she "was condemned."

She should have used her words to neutralize her troubles instead of to multiply them.

For example – had she said repeatedly: "I cast every burden upon the Christ within and I go free," and not voiced her sorrows, they would have faded from her life, for *"by your words you are justified."*

* * * * *

"I will give to thee the land that thou *seest.*"

Man is ever reaping on the external what he has sown in his thought world.

For example: A woman needed money and was walking along the street making the affirmation that God was her immediate supply.

She looked down and at her feet was a two dollar bill, which she picked up.

A man standing near (a watchman in a building), said to her: "Lady, did you pick up some money? I thought it was a piece of chewing-gum paper. A lot of people walked over it, but *when you came it opened up like a leaf."*

The others, thinking lack, had passed over it, but at her words of faith it unfurled.

So with the opportunities in life – one man sees, another passes by.

* * * * *

"Faith without works (or action) is dead."

The student, in order to bring into manifestation the answer to his prayer must show *active faith.*

For example: A woman came to me asking me to speak the word for the renting of a room.

I gave her the statement: "I give thanks that the room is now rented to the right and perfect man for the right price, giving perfect satisfaction."

Several weeks elapsed but the room had not been rented.

I asked: "Have you shown active faith? Have you followed every hunch in regard to the room?" She replied: "I had a hunch to get a lamp for the room, but I decided I couldn't afford it." I said: "You'll never rent the room until you get the lamp, for in buying the lamp you are *acting your faith*, impressing the subconscious mind with *certainty."*

I asked: "What is the price of the lamp?" She answered: "Four dollars." I exclaimed: "Four dollars standing between you and the perfect man!"

She became so enthusiastic, she bought *two* lamps.

About a week elapsed and in walked the perfect man. He did not smoke and paid the rent in advance and fulfilled her ideal in every way.

Unless you become as a little child and dig your ditches you shall in no wise enter the Kingdom of manifestation.

(See *The Game of Life and How to Play It*.)

* * * * *

"Without the vision my people perish." Unless man has some objective, some Promised Land to look forward to, he begins to perish.

We see it so often in small country towns, in the men who sit around a stove all winter, who "Ain't got no ambition."

Within each one is an undiscovered country, a gold mine.

I knew a man in a country town called "Magnolia Charlie," because he always found the first magnolia in the spring.

He was a shoemaker, but every afternoon left his work to go to the station to meet the four-fifteen train, from a distant city.

They were the only romances in his life, the first magnolia and the four-fifteen train.

He felt vaguely the call of the vision in the superconscious mind.

No doubt, the Divine Design for him included travel and perhaps he was to become a genius in the plant world.

Through the spoken word the Divine Design may be released and each one fulfill his destiny.

"I now see clearly the perfect plan of my life. Divine enthusiasm fires me and I now fulfill my destiny."

The Spiritual attitude towards money is to know that God *is man's supply*, and that he draws it from the abundance of the spheres, through his faith and spoken word.

When man realizes this he loses all greed for money, and is fearless in letting it go out.

With his magic purse of the Spirit, his supply is *endless* and *immediate*, and he knows also that *giving* precedes *receiving*.

For example: "A woman came to me asking me to speak the word for five hundred dollars by the first of August. (It was then about the first of July.)

I knew her very well, and said: "The trouble with you is you don't *give* enough. You must open your channels of supply by *giving*."

She had accepted an invitation to visit a friend and did not want to go on account of the formality.

She said: "Please treat me to be polite for three weeks, and I want to get away as soon as possible, and be sure to speak the word for the five hundred dollars."

She went to the friend's house, was unhappy and restless and tried continually to leave, but was always persuaded to stay longer.

She remembered my advice, however, and gave the people about her presents. Whenever possible she made a little gift.

It was nearing the first of August and no signs of the five hundred dollars, and no way of escape from the visit.

The last day of July she said: "Oh God! maybe I haven't given enough!" So she tipped all the servants more than she had intended.

The first of August, her hostess said to her: "My dear, I want to make you a gift," and she handed her a check for five hundred dollars!

God works in unexpected ways his wonders to perform.

* * * * *

AFFIRMATIONS

God is incapable of separation or division; therefore, my good is incapable of separation or division. I am *one* with my undivided good.

* * * * *

All that is mine by Divine Right is now released and reaches me in a perfect way under Grace.

* * * * *

God's work is finished now and must manifest.

* * * * *

I serve only faith and my unlimited abundance is made manifest.

* * * * *

I am undisturbed by appearances. I trust in God – and He now brings to me the desires of my heart.

* * * * *

My good now overtakes me in a surprising way.

* * * * *

The Divine Plan of my life cannot be tampered with. It is incorruptible and indestructible. It awaits only my recognition.

* * * * *

There is no there – there is only here.

* * * * *

Reveal to me the way, let me see clearly the blessing which Thou hast given me.

* * * * *

Let Thy blessed will be done in me this day.

* * * * *

Hunches are my hounds of Heaven – they lead me in the perfect way.

* * * * *

All things I seek are now seeking me.

* * * * *

Divine Activity is now operating in my mind, body and affairs, whether I see it or not.

* * * * *

Since I am one with the Only Presence, I am one with my heart's desire.

* * * * *

I now have the single eye of the Spirit and see only completion.

* * * * *

I am a perfect idea in Divine Mind and I am always in my right place doing my right work at the right time for the right pay.

* * * * *

The Columbus in you will see you through.

* * * * *

I am an irresistible magnet for checks, bills and currency – for everything that belongs to me by Divine Right.

* * * * *

Thou in me art completion. As I have asked I must receive.

* * * * *

The law of God is the law of increase and I give thanks for increase under grace in perfect ways.

* * * * *

I dwell in a sea of abundance. I see clearly my inexhaustible supply. I see clearly just what to do.

* * * * *

My "World of the Wondrous" now swings into manifestation and I enter my Promised Land under grace!

Great peace have I who love thy law of nonresistance and nothing shall offend me.

* * * * *

Thou in me art Inspiration, Revelation and Illumination.

Conclusion

Nothing is too good
to be true
Nothing is too wonderful
to happen
Nothing is too good
to last

CONCLUSION

CHOOSE THE AFFIRMATION which appeals to you the most and *wave it over the situation which confronts you.*

It is your *magic wand*, for your *word* is God in *action*.

"It shall not return unto me void but shall accomplish that whereunto it is sent." (Isaiah 55-11.)

"But I say, have they not heard? Yes, verily, their sound went into all the earth and *their words unto the end of the world.*" (Romans 10-18.)

REVIVE *classics*

"There is no friend as loyal as a book." Ernest Hemingway

1984 BY GEORGE ORWELL
20,000 Leagues Under the Sea BY JULES VERNE
A Christmas Carol BY CHARLES DICKENS
A Christmas Carol and Other Christmas Stories BY CHARLES DICKENS
A Connecticut Yankee in King Arthur's Court BY MARK TWAIN
A Doll's House BY HENRIK IBSEN
A Fighting Man of Mars BY EDGAR RICE BURROUGHS
A Hero of Our Time BY MIKHAIL LERMONTOV
A History of New York BY WASHINGTON IRVING
A Little Princess BY FRANCES HODGSON BURNETT
A Journal of the Plague Year BY DANIEL DEFOE
A Passage to India BY E. M. FORSTER
A Portrait of the Artist as a Young Man BY JAMES JOYCE
A Princess of Mars BY EDGAR RICE BURROUGHS
A Room with a View BY E. M. FORSTER
A Study in Scarlet BY ARTHUR CONAN DOYLE
A Tale of Two Cities BY CHARLES DICKENS
Aesop's Fables BY AESOP
Against Nature (A Rebours) BY JORIS-KARL HUYSMANS
Agnes Grey BY ANNE BRONTË
Alice in Wonderland BY LEWIS CARROLL
All Quiet on the Western Front BY ERICH MARIA REMARQUE
American Indian Stories & Old Indian Legends BY ZITKÁLA-ŠÁ
An American Tragedy BY THEODORE DREISER
Anabasis BY XENOPHON
Animal Farm BY GEORGE ORWELL
Anna Karenina BY LEO TOLSTOY
Anne of Avonlea BY LUCY MAUD MONTGOMERY
Anne of Green Gables BY LUCY MAUD MONTGOMERY
Anthem BY AYN RAND
Apologia Pro Vita Sua BY JOHN HENRY NEWMAN
Around the World in 80 Days BY JULES VERNE
As a Man Thinketh BY JAMES ALLEN
Au Bonheur des Dames BY ÉMILE ZOLA
Autobiography of a Yogi BY PARAMAHANSA YOGANANDA
Barnaby Rudge BY CHARLES DICKENS
Bel-Ami BY GUY DE MAUPASSANT
Ben-Hur BY LEW WALLACE
Beowulf in Verse and in Prose BY ANONYMOUS, E. KIRTLAN & J. HALL
Beyond Good and Evil BY FRIEDRICH NIETZSCHE
Billy Budd, Sailor BY HERMAN MELVILLE
Black Beauty BY ANNA SEWELL
Bleak House BY CHARLES DICKENS
Candide BY VOLTAIRE
Captain Blood BY RAFAEL SABATINI
Captains Courageous BY RUDYARD KIPLING
Catiline's War, and The Jurgurthine War BY SALLUST
Common Sense BY THOMAS PAINE
Confessions of an English Opium-Eater BY THOMAS DE QUINCEY
Count Magnus and Other Ghost Stories BY M. R. JAMES

Cousin Bette BY HONORÉ DE BALZAC
Cranford BY ELIZABETH GASKELL
Crime and Punishment BY FYODOR DOSTOEVSKY
Daphnis and Chloe BY LONGUS
Dark Night of the Soul BY ST. JOHN OF THE CROSS
David Copperfield BY CHARLES DICKENS
Dead Souls BY NIKOLAI GOGOL
Death Comes for the Archbishop BY WILLA CATHER
Democracy in America BY ALEXIS DE TOCQUEVILLE
Devils BY FYODOR DOSTOEVSKY
Dialogues Concerning Natural Religion BY DAVID HUME
Discourse on the Origin of Inequality BY JEAN-JACQUES ROUSSEAU
Discourse on Method & Meditations on First Philosophy BY RENÉ DESCARTES
Doctor Thorne BY ANTHONY TROLLOPE
Dombey and Son BY CHARLES DICKENS
Don Quixote BY MIGUEL DE CERVANTES
Dracula BY BRAM STOKER
Dubliners BY JAMES JOYCE
Ecclesiastical History of the English People BY BEDE
Emily of New Moon BY LUCY MAUD MONTGOMERY
Emma BY JANE AUSTEN
Ethan Frome BY EDITH WHARTON
Eugene Onegin BY ALEXANDER PUSHKIN
Eugénie Grandet (The Human Comedy) BY HONORÉ DE BALZAC
Evelina BY FRANCES BURNEY
Far from the Madding Crowd BY THOMAS HARDY
Fathers and Sons BY IVAN TURGENEV
Fear and Trembling BY SOREN KIERKEGAARD
Five Children and It BY E. NESBIT
Five Dialogues: Euthyphro, Apology, Crito, Meno, Phaedo BY PLATO
Flatland BY EDWIN A. ABBOTT
Frankenstein BY MARY SHELLEY
From the Earth to the Moon BY JULES VERNE
Gargantua and Pantagruel BY FRANCOIS RABELAIS
Gone with the Wind BY MARGARET MITCHELL
Gorgias BY PLATO
Grace Abounding to the Chief of Sinners BY JOHN BUNYAN
Great Expectations BY CHARLES DICKENS
Grimm's Fairy Tales BY JAKOB AND WILHELM GRIMM
Gulliver's Travels BY JONATHAN SWIFT
Guy Mannering BY SIR WALTER SCOTT
Hamlet BY WILLIAM SHAKESPEARE
Hans Christian Andersen's Fairy Tales BY HANS CHRISTIAN ANDERSEN
Hard Times BY CHARLES DICKENS
Heart of Darkness BY JOSEPH CONRAD
Heidi BY JOHANNA SPYRI
Hellenica BY XENOPHON
History of the Decline & Fall of the Roman Empire Vol 1&2 BY E. GIBBON
History of the Decline & Fall of the Roman Empire Vol 3&4 BY E. GIBBON
History of the Decline & Fall of the Roman Empire Vol 5&6 BY E. GIBBON

REVIVE classics

"If a book is well written, I always find it too short." Jane Austen

How to Grow Old and a Guide to Friendship by Cicero
Howards End by E. M. Forster
Idylls of the King by Alfred Lord Tennyson
In Our Time by Ernest Hemingway
Incidents in the Life of a Slave Girl by Harriet Jacobs
Interior Castle by St. Teresa of Avila
Ivanhoe by Sir Walter Scott
Jane Eyre by Charlotte Brontë
Journey to the Center of the Earth by Jules Verne
Jude the Obscure by Thomas Hardy
Just So Stories by Rudyard Kipling
Kidnapped by Robert Louis Stevenson
Kim by Rudyard Kipling
King Solomon's Mines by H. Rider Haggard
Lady Audley's Secret by Mary Elizabeth Braddon
Lady Chatterley's Lover by D. H. Lawrence
Le Morte d'Arthur: by Sir Thomas Malory
Leaves of Grass by Walt Whitman
Les Misérables by Victor Hugo
Letters from a Stoic by Lucius Annaeus Seneca
Leviathan by Thomas Hobbes
Little Dorrit by Charles Dickens
Little Lord Fauntleroy by Frances Hodgson Burnett
Little Men by Louisa May Alcott
Little Women by Louisa May Alcott
Looking Backward by Edward Bellamy
Macbeth by William Shakespeare
Madame Bovary by Gustave Flaubert
Maggie A Girl of the Streets by Stephen Crane
Main Street by Sinclair Lewis
Mansfield Park by Jane Austen
Martin Chuzzlewit by Charles Dickens
Martin Eden by Jack London
Meditations by Marcus Aurelius
Memoirs of General W. T. Sherman by William T. Sherman
Memorabilia by Xenophon
Middlemarch by George Eliot
Moby Dick by Herman Melville
Moll Flanders by Daniel Defoe
Mrs. Dalloway by Virginia Woolf
My Ántonia by Willa Cather
My Bondage and My Freedom by Frederick Douglass
Narrative of the Life of Frederick Douglass by Frederick Douglass
Nicholas Nickleby by Charles Dickens
Nicomachean Ethics by Aristotle
North and South by Elizabeth Gaskell
Northanger Abbey by Jane Austen
Notes from the Underground by Fyodor Dostoyevsky
O Pioneers! by Willa Cather
Oliver Twist by Charles Dickens

On Liberty by John Stuart Mill
On the Incarnation of the Word by Saint Athanasius
On War by Carl von Clausewitz
One of Ours by Willa Cather
Orlando by Virginia Woolf
Orthodoxy by Gilbert K. Chesterton
Our Mutual Friend by Charles Dickens
Paradise Lost by John Milton
Parmenides by Plato
Pensees by Blaise Pascal
Personal Recollections of Joan of Arc by Mark Twain
Persuasion by Jane Austen
Peter Pan by J. M. Barrie
Phantastes by George MacDonald
Pinocchio by Carlo Collodi
Plato: Five Dialogues by Plato
Plutarch's Lives by Plutarch
Poirot Investigates by Agatha Christie
Politics by Aristotle
Pollyanna by Eleanor H. Porter
Praise of Folly by Desiderius Erasmus
Pride & Prejudice by Jane Austen
Raggedy Ann Stories by Johnny Gruelle
Revelations of Divine Love by Julian of Norwich
Robinson Crusoe by Daniel Defoe
Second Treatise Of Government by John Locke
Self-Reliance, Nature, and Other Essays by Ralph Waldo Emerson
Sense & Sensibility by Jane Austen
Shirley by Charlotte Brontë
Silas Marner by George Eliot
Sister Carrie by Theodore Dreiser
Sons and Lovers by D. H. Lawrence
Swann's Way, In Search of Lost Time by Marcel Proust
Symposium by Plato
Tales from Shakespeare by Charles Lamb and Mary Lamb
Tao Te Ching by Laozi, translated by James Legge
Tarzan of the Apes by Edgar Rice Burroughs
Tess of the d'Urbervilles by Thomas Hardy
The Adventures of Huckleberry Finn by Mark Twain
The Adventures of Sherlock Holmes by Arthur Conan Doyle
The Adventures of Tom Sawyer by Mark Twain
The Age of Innocence by Edith Wharton
The Agricola and Germania by Tacitus
The Alexiad by Anna Comnena
The Analects of Confucius by Confucius
The Antichrist by Friedrich Nietzsche
The Apocrypha: The Complete Deuterocanonical Books of the Bible
The Art of War by Sun Tzu
The Athenian Constitution by Aristotle
The Autobiography of an Ex-Colored Man by James Weldon Johnson

REVIVE classics

"A room without books is like a body without a soul." Cicero

The Autobiography of Benjamin Franklin BY BENJAMIN FRANKLIN
The Awakening BY KATE CHOPIN
The Beautiful and the Damned BY F. SCOTT FITZGERALD
The Bhagavad Gita BY VYASA
The Big Four BY AGATHA CHRISTIE
The Blazing World BY MARGARET CAVENDISH
The Blue Fairy Book BY ANDREW LANG
The Book of Enoch BY ENOCH
The Book of Jubilees BY ANONYMOUS
The Book of Mormon BY JOSEPH SMITH JR.
The Bridge of San Luis Rey BY THORNTON WILDER
The Brontë Sisters Collection BY CHARLOTTE, EMILY AND ANNE BRONTË
The Brothers Karamazov BY FYODOR DOSTOEVSKY
The Call of the Wild BY JACK LONDON
The Campaigns of Alexander BY ARRIAN
The Castle of Otranto BY HORACE WALPOLE
The Cat of Bubastes: A Tale of Ancient Egypt BY G. A HENTY
The Chessmen of Mars BY EDGAR RICE BURROUGHS
The City of God BY SAINT AUGUSTINE
The Civil War BY JULIUS CAESAR
The Communist Manifesto BY KARL MARX & FRIEDRICH ENGELS
The Complete Essays of Michel de Montaigne BY MICHEL DE MONTAIGNE
The Complete Essays of Plutarch BY PLUTARCH
The Complete Heimskringla BY SNORRI STURLUSON
The Complete Journals of Lewis and Clark BY M. LEWIS & W. CLARK
The Complete Personal Memoirs of Ulysses S. Grant BY ULYSSES S. GRANT
The Complete Wizard of Oz Collection BY FRANK L. BAUM
The Complete Works of H. P. Lovecraft BY H. P. LOVECRAFT
The Complete Works of Horace BY HORACE
The Confessions of Saint Augustine BY SAINT AUGUSTINE OF HIPPO
The Consolation of Philosophy BY BOETHIUS
The Constitution of the United States of America BY VARIOUS
The Corpus Hermeticum BY HERMES TRISMEGISTUS
The Count of Monte Cristo BY ALEXANDRE DUMAS
The Country of the Pointed Firs BY SARAH ORNE JEWETT
The Decameron BY GIOVANNI BOCCACCIO
The Decline and Fall of the Roman Empire Vol 1 & 2 BY EDWARD GIBBON
The Decline and Fall of the Roman Empire Vol 3 & 4 BY EDWARD GIBBON
The Decline and Fall of the Roman Empire Vol 5 & 6 BY EDWARD GIBBON
The Deerslayer BY JAMES FENIMORE COOPER
The Dhammapada BY BUDDHA
The Discourses BY NICCOLÒ MACHIAVELLI
The Discourses of Epictetus BY EPICTETUS
The Divine Comedy - Inferno, Purgatorio, Paradiso BY DANTE
The Education of Henry Adams BY HENRY ADAMS
The Enchanted April BY ELIZABETH VON ARNIM
The Everlasting Man BY GILBERT K. CHESTERTON
The Federalist Papers BY A. HAMILTON, J. MADISON & J. JAY
The First Men in the Moon BY H. G. WELLS
The Fortune of the Rougons BY ÉMILE ZOLA

The Gallic War BY JULIUS CAESAR
The Game of Life and How to Play It BY FLORENCE SCOVEL SHINN
The Genealogy of Morals BY FRIEDRICH NIETZSCHE
The Gods of Mars BY EDGAR RICE BURROUGHS
The Golden Ass BY APULEIUS
The Golden Bowl BY HENRY JAMES
The Good Soldier BY FORD MADOX FORD
The Great Gatsby BY F. SCOTT FITZGERALD
The Great God Pan and The White People BY ARTHUR MACHEN
The Histories BY HERODOTUS
The History of Rome: Books 1-10 BY TITUS LIVY
The History of Rome: Books 21-30 BY TITUS LIVY
The History of Rome: Books 31-45 BY TITUS LIVY
The History of the Church BY EUSEBIUS
The History of the Franks BY GREGORY OF TOURS
The History of the Peloponnesian War BY THUCYDIDES
The Hound of the Baskervilles BY ARTHUR CONAN DOYLE
The House of Mirth BY EDITH WHARTON
The House of the Seven Gables BY NATHANIEL HAWTHORNE
The Hunchback of Notre-Dame BY VICTOR HUGO
The Idiot BY FYODOR DOSTOEVSKY
The Iliad BY HOMER
The Imitation of Christ BY THOMAS À KEMPIS
The Importance of Being Earnest BY OSCAR WILDE
The Innocents Abroad BY MARK TWAIN
The Interesting Narrative of the Life of Olaudah Equiano BY O. EQUIANO
The Invisible Man BY H. G. WELLS
The Island of Doctor Moreau BY H. G. WELLS
The Jungle BY UPTON SINCLAIR
The Jungle Book BY RUDYARD KIPLING
The Kama Sutra BY VĀTSYĀYANA
The King in Yellow BY ROBERT W. CHAMBERS
The King James Bible - The New Testament BY THE KING JAMES BIBLE
The King James Bible - The Old Testament BY THE KING JAMES BIBLE
The Kybalion BY THREE INITIATES
The Lady of the Camellias BY ALEXANDRE DUMAS
The Lais of Marie de France BY MARIE DE FRANCE
The Last Man BY MARY SHELLEY
The Last of the Mohicans BY JAMES FENIMORE COOPER
The Law and the Lady BY WILKIE COLLINS
The Legend of Sleepy Hollow BY WASHINGTON IRVING
The Letters of Abelard and Heloise BY H. D'ARGENTEUIL & P. ABELARD
The Letters of Pliny the Younger BY PLINY THE YOUNGER
The Life and Opinions of Tristram Shandy BY LAURENCE STERNE
The Light Princess BY GEORGE MACDONALD
The Longest Journey BY E. M. FORSTER
The Lost World BY ARTHUR CONAN DOYLE
The Mabinogion BY ANONYMOUS
The Man in the Brown Suit BY AGATHA CHRISTIE
The Man in the Iron Mask BY ALEXANDRE DUMAS

REVIVE classics

"The man who doesn't read has no advantage over the man who can't read." Mark Twain

The Man Who Was Thursday BY GILBERT K. CHESTERTON
The Master Mind of Mars BY EDGAR RICE BURROUGHS
The Mayor of Casterbridge BY THOMAS HARDY
The Memoirs of Sherlock Holmes BY ARTHUR CONAN DOYLE
The Merry Adventures of Robin Hood BY HOWARD PYLE
The Metamorphosis BY FRANZ KAFKA
The Mill on the Floss BY GEORGE ELIOT
The Monk: A Romance BY MATTHEW LEWIS
The Moonstone BY WILKIE COLLINS
The Murder of Roger Ackroyd BY AGATHA CHRISTIE
The Murder on the Links BY AGATHA CHRISTIE
The Mysterious Affair at Styles BY AGATHA CHRISTIE
The Mysterious Island BY JULES VERNE
The Mystery of Edwin Drood BY CHARLES DICKENS
The Mystery of the Blue Train BY AGATHA CHRISTIE
The Nature of Things BY TITUS LUCRETIUS CARUS
The Odyssey BY HOMER
The Old Curiosity Shop BY CHARLES DICKENS
The Origin of Species BY CHARLES DARWIN
The Painted Veil BY W. SOMERSET MAUGHAM
The Phantom of the Opera BY GASTON LEROUX
The Pickwick Papers BY CHARLES DICKENS
The Picture of Dorian Gray BY OSCAR WILDE
The Portrait of a Lady BY HENRY JAMES
The Prince BY NICCOLÒ MACHIAVELLI
The Prince and the Pauper BY MARK TWAIN
The Princess and Curdie BY GEORGE MACDONALD
The Princess and the Goblin BY GEORGE MACDONALD
The Problems of Philosophy BY BERTRAND RUSSELL
The Prophet BY KAHLIL GIBRAN
The Pursuit of God BY A. W. TOZER
The Railway Children BY E. NESBIT
The Rainbow BY D. H. LAWRENCE
The Red Badge of Courage BY STEPHEN CRANE
The Republic BY PLATO
The Return of Sherlock Holmes BY SIR ARTHUR CONAN DOYLE
The Return of the Native BY THOMAS HARDY
The Richest Man In Babylon BY GEORGE S CLASON
The Rough Riders BY THEODORE ROOSEVELT
The Rule of Saint Benedict BY SAINT BENEDICT
The Scarlet Letter BY NATHANIEL HAWTHORNE
The Scarlet Pimpernel BY BARONESS ORCZY
The Science of Getting Rich BY WALLACE D. WATTLES
The Sea-Wolf BY JACK LONDON
The Secret Adversary BY AGATHA CHRISTIE
The Secret Garden BY FRANCES HODGSON BURNETT
The Secret of Chimneys BY AGATHA CHRISTIE
The Sign of the Four BY ARTHUR CONAN DOYLE
The Social Contract BY JEAN-JACQUES ROUSSEAU
The Song of the Lark BY WILLA CATHER

The Sorrows Of Young Werther BY JOHANN WOLFGANG VON GOETHE
The Souls of Black Folk BY W. E. B. DU BOIS
The Strange Case of Dr. Jekyll & Mr. Hyde BY ROBERT LOUIS STEVENSON
The Story of a Soul: The Autobiography of SAINT THÉRÈSE OF LISIEUX
The Sun Also Rises BY ERNEST HEMINGWAY
The Swiss Family Robinson BY JOHANN DAVID WYSS
The Tale of Peter Rabbit BY BEATRIX POTTER
The Tarzan Collection BY EDGAR RICE BURROUGHS
The Tenant of Wildfell Hall BY ANNE BRONTË
The Theory of Moral Sentiments BY ADAM SMITH
The Three Musketeers BY ALEXANDRE DUMAS
The Time Machine BY H. G. WELLS
The Turn of the Screw BY HENRY JAMES
The Twelve Caesars BY SUETONIUS
The Upanishads BY ANONYMOUS
The Valley of Fear BY ARTHUR CONAN DOYLE
The Varieties of Religious Experience BY WILLIAM JAMES
The War of the Worlds BY H. G. WELLS
The Warlord of Mars BY EDGAR RICE BURROUGHS
The Wealth of Nations BY ADAM SMITH
The Wind in the Willows BY KENNETH GRAHAME
The Wizard of Oz BY L. FRANK BAUM
The Woman in White BY WILKIE COLLINS
The Yoga Sutras OF PATANJALI
Theodore Roosevelt: An Autobiography BY THEODORE ROOSEVELT
Theogony and Works and Days BY HESIOD
Thérèse Raquin BY ÉMILE ZOLA
This Side of Paradise BY F. SCOTT FITZGERALD
Through the Looking-Glass BY LEWIS CARROLL
Thuvia, Maid of Mars BY EDGAR RICE BURROUGHS
Timaeus and Critias BY PLATO
To the Lighthouse BY VIRGINIA WOOLF
Tom Jones BY HENRY FIELDING
Treasure Island BY ROBERT LOUIS STEVENSON
Twelve Years a Slave BY SOLOMON NORTHUP
Ulysses BY JAMES JOYCE
Uncle Tom's Cabin BY HARRIET BEECHER STOWE
Up From Slavery BY BOOKER T. WASHINGTON
Utilitarianism BY JOHN STUART MILL
Utopia BY SIR THOMAS MORE
Vanity Fair BY WILLIAM MAKEPEACE THACKERAY
Villette BY CHARLOTTE BRONTË
Walden BY HENRY DAVID THOREAU
War and Peace BY LEO TOLSTOY
We BY YEVGENY ZAMYATIN
What's Wrong with the World BY GILBERT K. CHESTERTON
White Fang BY JACK LONDON
White Nights and The Gambler BY FYODOR DOSTOEVSKY
Women in Love BY D. H. LAWRENCE
Wuthering Heights BY EMILY BRONTË

Milton Keynes UK
Ingram Content Group UK Ltd.
UKHW031401011224
451790UK00014B/177/J